LIVING
as United Methodist
Christians

LIVING
AS
United Methodist Christians

Our Story,
Our Beliefs,
Our Lives

ANDY & SALLY
LANGFORD

Abingdon Press
Nashville

LIVING AS UNITED METHODIST CHRISTIANS
OUR STORY, OUR BELIEFS, OUR LIVES

Copyright © 2011 by Abingdon Press

This book is printed on acid-free paper

Library of Congress Cataloging-in-Publication Data

Langford, Andy.
   Living as United Methodist Christians : our story, our beliefs, our lives / Andy and Sally Langford.
       p.   cm.
   ISBN 978-1-4267-1193-0 (alk. paper)
   1. United Methodist Church (U.S.)   I. Langford, Sally.   II. Title.
   BX8331.3.L36 2011
   230'.76—dc22

                                                                          2010048805

Scripture quotations are from the Common English Bible. Copyright © 2011 by the Common English Bible. All rights reserved. Used by permission. (www.CommonEnglish Bible.com)

Excerpts from *The Book of Discipline of The United Methodist Church*, copyright © 2008 by The United Methodist Publishing House, are used by permission.

11 12 13 14 15 16 17 18 19 20—10 9 8 7 6 5 4 3 2 1

MANUFACTURED IN THE UNITED STATES OF AMERICA

CONTENTS

Words of Welcome from the Editor 7

Words of Welcome from the Authors 9

1. What Is Our Biblical Story? 13

2. What Do We Share with Other Christians? 27

3. What Is Our United Methodist Story? 41

4. What Do United Methodists Believe? 57

5. How Do United Methodists Serve God
   and Neighbor? 71

6. How Do United Methodists Live
   and Worship? 87

If You Want to Know More 103

Leader Helps for a Small-Group Study 105

WORDS

OF

WELCOME

FROM THE

EDITOR

The United Methodist Publishing House offers many fine resources to help people learn more about the history, organization, and beliefs of The United Methodist Church as part of preparing for membership. We have also received requests for resources that will help people not only learn *about* The United Methodist Church but that will, in addition, *inspire them to claim for themselves* the redemptive love of God revealed through Jesus Christ as part of their entry into membership in United Methodist congregations. *Living as United Methodist Christians: Our Story, Our Beliefs, Our Lives* will help adults hear and claim for themselves the Christian story, the particular emphases of belief and practice of United Methodist Christians, and ways individuals and communities live and worship as United Methodist Christians.

We are excited to offer a book that is designed to inspire and engage anyone who wants to know how United Methodists live their lives as followers of Jesus Christ. *Living as United Methodist Christians* can be used for individual reading and reflection, for small-group study, or for retreat settings. In each chapter, you will find well-written content that is easy to understand and re-flection questions that will help people engage the material with their heads and with their hearts. Leaders who want to use the book for small groups or retreats will find a concise leader guide at the end of the book. The book also contains an invitation to read and reflect upon the membership vows, to unite with a local congregation of The United Methodist Church, and to live as a United Methodist Christian.

Pamela Dilmore, Editor

WORDS

OF

WELCOME FROM
THE AUTHORS

In 1784, John Wesley gathered three pastors on the coast of England and sent them to North America with a challenge. Arming them with a passion for evangelism, a set of rules for holy living, a list of theological affirmations, and a prayerbook entitled *The Sunday Service of the Methodists in North America*, Wesley charged Thomas Coke, Richard Whatcoat, and Thomas Vasey to journey to the unchurched United States of America and "offer them Christ."

At Christmas in Baltimore, Maryland, Coke, Whatcoat, and Vasey ordained thirteen preachers and consecrated two bishops to form The United Methodist Episcopal Church. The new church was the first indigenous denomination in the newly forming United States of America. A flame that began in a rural English parish spread to a Bible study at Oxford, jumped next to a small meetinghouse in London, crossed the Atlantic Ocean, and then continued to spread like wildfire across the world. Today over seventy-five million people in a variety of denominations across our planet are spiritual heirs of John Wesley.

Over eleven million direct heirs of these Christian disciples from the eighteenth century now call themselves United Methodist Christians. We are still responding to Wesley's challenge to offer Jesus Christ to women, children, and men in over 132 countries. In a mission congregation in the sands of Dubai, a small Appalachian chapel, a storefront church on top of a trash dump in Manila, a great university in Zimbabwe, a congregation in an abandoned factory in Moscow, a small chapel on Wall Street in New York City, a mission congregation in the tenderloin district of San Francisco, a megachurch in Houston, and almost 42,000 other congregations around the world, the flame continues to burn. We are all United Methodists!

So how do we describe United Methodists? Where do we come from? What do we believe? How do United Methodists act? What are our distinctive characteristics? What is required to be a member of our denomination? How do we grow as disciples of Jesus Christ within this great communion? In this resource, we offer answers to these questions and others in broad, impressionistic strokes as we describe the ethos of our distinctive United Methodist culture. We invite you to explore with us who we are as United Methodist Christians. We will introduce you to how United Methodists live, think, and act as followers of Jesus Christ.

Some of you, like Andy, have been members of The United Methodist Church since your birth. Others of you, like Sally, joined our denomination to become a part of a welcoming congregation and to align yourselves with our theology and mission. And others of you are not members, but want to know more about United Methodists. You may have grown up in another faith tradition, or you may come to this study without any religious background at all. You may have married into this denomination, or you may be looking for a place of worship and service where every member of your family can find a home. You may be here because of a life-altering change—the death of a loved one, a move to a new town, or the religious questions of your child that you cannot answer. Whoever you are, welcome to The United Methodist Church!

The United Methodist Church possesses the characteristics of many other Christian traditions, but it has its own distinctions. Our denomination combines knowledge and vital piety, believing that serious theological reflection and spiritual practices are both part of the Christian life. United Methodists link personal and social holiness, expecting high personal integrity and deep concern for social justice. We are both evangelical and sacramental, showing concern for people who have not accepted Jesus Christ as Savior and honoring the transforming power of baptism and Holy Communion. United Methodists are also both local and connectional, expressing our faith in local congregations, in regional associations, and in global missions, so that we might do more together than any of us could do separately.

We, Sally and Andy, are proud to be United Methodists. Andy's family has been Methodist over 150 years, through at least through six generations. Andy owns an 1865 Methodist hymnal in German, which belonged to his great-great-grandmother in Indiana. Sally grew up in a Southern Baptist congregation but then joined Colliers United Methodist Church where she served as a summer ministerial intern. This small membership congregation in the Appalachian foothills loved her into The United Methodist Church. Our denomination has blessed us in many ways. The United Methodist Church has paid our salaries, provided parsonages for our housing, nurtured our daughters, introduced us to Christians around the world, and most important, shaped our spiritual formation as disciples of Jesus Christ. We are who we are because of The United Methodist Church.

We invite you to claim for yourself the continuing story of God's mighty acts of creation, redemption, and power through Jesus Christ within The United Methodist Church. As you begin or continue to see yourself within this living, dynamic part of the universal body of Jesus Christ, we invite you to identify some new ways to live and grow as a United Methodist Christian.

Andy and Sally Langford

1. What Is
Our Biblical Story?

*United Methodist Christians affirm the authority of the
Holy Bible as the source of our understanding about God
and God's relationship with us.*

*"Every scripture is inspired by God and is useful for teaching, for
showing mistakes, for correcting, and for training character, so that
the person who belongs to God can be equipped to do everything
that is good."*

2 TIMOTHY 3:16-17

The Bible Moths

In 1729, three young men at Oxford University gathered together in a dorm room to read the Bible. These seekers then invited a twenty-three-year-old professor and newly ordained priest
in the Church of England to lead their Bible study for the next six
years. The bright, intense scholar was John Wesley. Around the
raucous university town, other students called the group "Bible
Moths," because they hovered over the Scriptures like moths
around a flame. Another name, based on their methodical pattern
of biblical study, prayer, fasting, and service stuck: Methodists.
John Wesley distributed a pamphlet entitled "The Character of a
Methodist," in which he described the people called Methodist:

The distinguishing marks of Methodists are not their opinions of any sort. Their assenting to this or that scheme of religion, embracing any particular set of notions, espousing the judgment of one person or of another, are all quite wide of the point.... We believe the written word of God to be the only and sufficient rule both of Christian faith and practice.... We believe Christ to be the eternal, supreme God.... But as to all opinions which do not strike at the root of Christianity, we think and let think. So that whatsoever they are, whether right or wrong, they are no distinguishing marks of Methodists.[1]

Wesley did not begin his ministry to create something unique. He neither advocated a peculiar way of being Christian nor intended to form a new Christian denomination. Wesley simply listened to the Bible and did what God commanded. Nevertheless, that gathering of eighteenth-century young adults, who studied the Bible and walked in the footsteps of Jesus, marked the beginning of a huge movement. Over the past two and a half centuries, this movement has changed millions of lives and transformed the world in significant ways.

> What is the role of the Holy Bible in your journey of Christian faith?

People of the Book

United Methodists are first and foremost people who read the Bible and seek to be disciples of Jesus Christ within the universal church. We are similar to the first followers of Jesus Christ as we draw near to Jesus, explore the riches of the Holy Scriptures, and know that our lives have been transformed. In the first decades following the death of Jesus, Christians gathered in homes around the Mediterranean Sea to tell stories about the risen Christ and read aloud the letters of traveling preachers like Paul. Similarly, Wesley first learned the stories of Jesus when his mother taught him to read through the pages of the Bible. Barbara Heck, a Methodist laywoman in New York City, in 1766 invited English immigrants and African slaves to her cottage to read the Bible and grow in their faith. And so the movement from which came The United Methodist Church grew.

This tradition of Bible study and faithful discipleship continues in our day and time throughout The United Methodist Church. In the Philippines, United Methodists gather each Sunday morning on top of a large trash dump in Manila to read the Bible and discern God's call to serve their neighbors. The same is true in countless other United Methodist congregations from Africa to Europe to the United States to Southeast Asia. Together with other Christians around the world, we are all children of God who listen for God's voice and seek to do God's will.

> What memories do you have about the Bible as you were growing up? How many Bibles do you own? How often do you read the Bible?

What Is the Bible?

United Methodists believe that the Bible is the primary source for hearing God's call on our lives. Our Bible contains sixty-six different books in the Old and New Testaments, which were written over a period of a thousand years but reflect events over a much longer period of time. Composed by many authors, the books of the Bible spoke to specific audiences in particular historical and sociological contexts. The human experiences depicted throughout the pages of the Bible are believably real and down to earth. People in the Bible are born, marry, have children, get sick, and die. These biblical characters also betray their friends; commit violent acts of rape, murder, and war; and put their own desires and interests before the needs and concerns of others.

Even so, Christians, including United Methodists, have affirmed over the ages that the Bible is the authoritative word of God for human beings. God's Spirit guided the Bible's authors as they compiled stories of God's actions in human history and reported on people who were transformed by God from self-centered individuals to obedient children of God. God's Spirit was also at work as the various writings were collected and then chosen to be part of the official Scriptures for the church universal. Furthermore, God's Spirit continues to move within human minds and hearts today whenever we read the Bible and hear God speaking to us. Whenever we allow the Holy Spirit to inform our reading and hearing of the Bible, then the ancient Scriptures confront us once again with God's life-changing word.

> Has the Bible spoken to you in a way that enriched your life? When? How? How might you create more time to prayerfully read and reflect on Bible passages?

What Does the Bible Teach?

From Genesis, the first book of the Bible, to the last book, Revelation, God reveals God's own self to us as the world's Creator, Redeemer, and Sustainer. At creation, God formed human beings in the image of God and breathed life into them. God placed humans in a beautiful world and called them into a loving relationship with God and all creation. The human beings were disobedient and were cast out of Eden. God continued to provide for them and to speak to them, yet over and over again, the biblical stories reveal that people sought to be self-sufficient and failed to love God and others.

In response, God continued to call people back into a right relationship with God and others. Abraham and Sarah were called to leave their native country, travel to a new land, and become a blessing to the nations. When God's people were slaves in Egypt, God sent Moses to set them free and to lead them again to the Promised Land. Spirit-filled men and women served God's people once they had crossed the Jordan River. God then granted the people's wish for rulers such as David and Solomon to establish an earthly kingdom. When the kings ruled unjustly, prophets arose to proclaim words of judgment and hope.

In the fullness of time, God sent Jesus Christ, born of Mary and the Holy Spirit. Jesus healed the sick, preached forgiveness and reconciliation, and proclaimed that a new reign of God had been initiated through him. Jesus brought together poor and rich, female and male, and diseased and healthy people and molded them into a new community. When Jesus' ministry among the people was rejected by the religious leaders and Roman officials, he was arrested and crucified. At its climax, the Bible proclaims that God raised Jesus from the dead. When Jesus the Christ ascended into heaven, the Holy Spirit became the guide and companion of his followers. Through the Holy Spirit, the church was formed, and its members shared with family, friends, and strangers the good news of life redeemed and abundant through Jesus Christ. Through the witness of Paul, Priscilla and Aquila, and others, the church spread from Jerusalem to Rome to the ends of the earth.

The Bible closes with the hope-filled vision of a new heaven and a new earth, in which God in Christ brings to fulfillment God's reign of peace and justice. At the end of history and in a new creation, all of God's people will live in harmony with God and one another. United Methodists, along with Christians everywhere, proclaim this scriptural message.

> Read Genesis 1–4; Exodus 3:1-17; Isaiah 11:1-9; Micah 6:8; Luke 4:16-10; John 3:16-17; Revelation 22:1-5. What do these scriptures say to you about God? about human beings? about God's relationship with human beings?

How Do United Methodists Read the Bible?

It is possible, of course, to read the Bible as a fascinating story-book. Engaging stories, such as Noah and the Ark, Esther in the court of King Ahasuerus, and Jesus' feeding of five thousand people with a lunch of bread and fish, fill the Bible. We also read the Bible to learn about ancient legal codes, hear beautiful poetry, and understand the history of Judaism and Christianity. United Methodists, however, are challenged to read the Bible for a much more profound reason. We are challenged to read or listen to the Bible's words with the expectation that we will encounter the living God and be transformed.

United Methodists do not regard the Bible as being without error in regard to history, science, or geography. We do not read only one translation of the Bible. We read the Bible as a trustworthy roadmap and compass, inviting us to discover in its pages an intimate relationship with God through Jesus Christ. Everything we need to know about God and our relationship with God we discover within the Bible. When we read and reflect on the Bible's words, the Holy Spirit stirs within us, and God reveals how we are called to be formed in the image of Jesus.

John Wesley always proclaimed that he was a "person of one book"—the Bible.[2] According to Wesley, God reveals through the biblical story "the way to heaven." For Wesley, "heaven" or "salvation" was much more than a place of eternal bliss; heaven and salvation are a restored relationship with God and all of God's creation, which may begin now and last forever. United Methodists today affirm, as Wesley did, that "the Holy Scriptures containeth all things necessary to salvation" and are "the primary source and criterion for Christian doctrine."[3]

What is your view of the Bible? How do you think it can be a roadmap or compass in your faith journey?

Reading and Listening to the Bible

Reading the Bible can be intimidating to anyone who first opens its pages. Do we begin at the beginning and read straight through, or is it better to pick one book of the Bible to read first? How do we start?

In Wesley's "Preface to Explanatory Notes upon the Old Testament" he outlined how Methodists should read the Bible.[4] Here we paraphrase Wesley's suggestions:

1. Set apart a little time every morning and evening.
2. Read a chapter out of the Old Testament and one out of the New Testament; or simply read a single chapter or part of one chapter.
3. Read this Scripture to discern God's will and with a desire to do God's will.
4. Before and after you read, pray that what you read may be written on your heart.
5. While you read, frequently pause to examine yourself, both with regard to your heart and life. And whatever you discern, put that insight to use immediately.

For some readers, it helps to begin with one of the four Gospels, perhaps the Gospel According to Mark. Many readers turn to a devotional guide such as *The Upper Room* or the well-known book *A Guide to Prayer for All God's People* by Rueben P. Job and Norman Shawchuck.

While we may read the Bible alone, our own individual insights are often not enough to understand God's word to us and others. We often can hear God more clearly when we read the Scriptures with other believers. Acts 8:26-40 tells of Philip's encounter with an Ethiopian official, who was reading aloud the prophet Isaiah. "Do you really understand what you are reading?" Philip asked. The Ethiopian replied, "Without someone to guide me, how could I?" (Acts 8:30-31). Philip sat beside the official and explained the words of Isaiah. As Philip told the Ethiopian about God's love revealed in the life, death, and resurrection of Jesus, the official's life was changed, and he was baptized that very day.

United Methodists today often read the Bible together and listen for helpful insights from one another. In small groups at a local United Methodist church, a friend's home, or a coffee shop, we read the Bible together and listen for a word from God for our lives. Andy's congregation hosted a Bible study called *Beginnings* at a local pub called "The George Washington Tavern." Over coffee and cold drinks, a group of adults read Scripture, asked their most profound questions of one another, and discovered new relationships with one another and Jesus Christ.

Reading the Bible is also central to United Methodist worship from Bible readings, to sermons, to music. While every United Methodist pastor uses the Bible for preaching, United Methodist preachers approach the Bible in different ways. Some preachers design their preaching and worship around the Revised Common Lectionary, a three-year sequence of biblical lessons used by many Christians around the world. Other pastors preach through a whole book of the Bible at a time, while still other preachers choose topical themes. All of these preachers, however, listen for God's voice in a particular passage of the Bible and discern God's call on them and their communities. United Methodist preachers then proclaim the connections they have discovered between the life stories of the people in their congregations and the biblical stories of God's redemptive work. In worship, the congregation will often recite or sing the psalms. Our hymns and contemporary praise choruses are based on Scripture.

> Make a list of ways you experience the Bible in your worship service. If you are not already reading the Bible every day, consider how you might allow time to do so. Consider using Wesley's guidelines for reading the Bible. Would a daily devotional guide be helpful to you? Would a Bible study group be helpful?

The Bible and the Wesleyan Quadrilateral

Noted Wesley scholar Albert Outler is credited with developing the phrase *Wesleyan Quadrilateral* to describe the principal elements John Wesley used to inform Christian faith: Scripture, Tradition, Experience, and Reason. The United Methodist Church looks to these elements as the principal sources and criteria for what we know about our faith and for the decisions we make according to our faith. They are described in *The Book of Discipline.*[5] While not mentioned by name in the Bible or by Wesley, the Quadrilateral describes the basic filters through which United Methodists interpret our Christian faith. Our United Methodist beliefs and practices are grounded in Scripture, informed by Christian Tradition, enlivened by Experience, and tested by Reason.

We begin by affirming that the Bible is the primary source or foundation for our understanding of the Christian faith. The Old and New Testaments are the unique and authoritative standards for Christian doctrine. Wesley sometimes referred to Methodism as "scriptural Christianity." United Methodists begin with Scripture but listen for God's word in the context of the other parts of the Quadrilateral.

United Methodists also look at Tradition as a source for understanding our faith. Our understanding of God does not start anew with each generation or each person. Wesley knew the importance of drawing on the knowledge of other interpreters to understand God's word within the Bible. Wesley often read ancient and contemporary biblical commentaries, a wide range of theologians, and even the scientific writings of his age, such as Benjamin Franklin's studies of electricity. Wesley's *Notes on the New Testament* continues to be one of our foundational theological documents.

In addition to Tradition, we bring to the task our own distinctive personal and communal Experiences. Experience authenticates the truths revealed in Scripture and illumined by Tradition.

When a West African United Methodist reads that the Old Testament prophet Amos was confronted in his rural setting by the prophets of foreign gods, she may understand anew the challenges she faces from animist teachings in her own isolated village. Inevitably, her response to the Scripture will be different from the response to that same biblical text by a United Methodist in Paris, France, or San Francisco, California. Each one of us must determine in our own setting and context how to follow Jesus faithfully when surrounded by competing religious claims. United Methodists cherish the different perspectives we bring to our reading and interpretation of the Bible.

Finally, we discover how God's word is challenging us to become more like Christ through the use of our God-given Reason. Although God's revelation and our Experiences of God's grace continually surpass the scope of Reason, we believe that God gave us minds, and we are expected to use them.

How do Scripture, Tradition, Experience, and Reason help you sort through issues of Christian faith? Which do you primarily use? What potential do you see in the use of Tradition, Experience, and Reason as you interpret the Scriptures?

The Biblical Message of God's Grace

For United Methodists, God's grace is the primary message of the Bible. Grace is the active love of God in the lives of human beings irrespective of their own merit. We do not earn God's grace. God's grace is evident throughout the Old Testament as steadfast love, mercy, and justice in spite of the disobedience of God's people. We see God's grace at work in the biblical witness to Jesus' life, death, and resurrection. As the gospel writer John explains it, the Word of God "became flesh and made his home among us.... From his fullness we have all received grace upon grace" (John 1:14, 16). By the grace revealed to us in Jesus, we humans are brought into a right relationship with God and enabled to grow in our love for God and others.

In spite of suffering, violence, and evil, United Methodists assert that God's grace is present everywhere and available to us. Through grace, God stirs up in us a desire to seek God, summons us to repentance, pardons us, claims us as new people in Christ, and gives us hope of life eternal. Through grace, we are empowered to be more and more like Christ and to go out to serve the world.

John Newton, who wrote the hymn "Amazing Grace," became a Christian by the influence of Wesley and his friends. The words on Newton's tombstone say it all: "John Newton, Clerk, Once an Infidel and Libertine, A servant of slaves in Africa, Was, by the rich mercy of our Lord and Saviour, JESUS CHRIST, Preserved, restored, pardoned, And appointed to preach the Faith He had long laboured to destroy."

Grace changed Kelia's life as she read and listened to Scripture in Andy's United Methodist congregation. Kelia did not grow up in a church, and most of her adult contacts with Christians had been negative. When she and her fiancé sought to be married, various pastors in town turned them away because this was not their first marriage. But one Christmas morning, Kelia came to an informal worship service and heard the story of the birth of Jesus in Nazareth. Over the next few years, she occasionally returned to worship, sat on the back row, and listened to Bible stories she had never heard before. Kelia then took a huge risk and signed up for a thirty-two-week Bible study called DISCIPLE. Using the model of John Wesley's Bible study in Oxford, Pastor Reta and lay leaders gathered the group weekly to discuss the Bible and its impact on their lives. In preparation for the group meeting, Kelia and the other seekers read the Bible every day and reflected in their journals on what God was saying to them. During those weeks of study, discussion, and reflection, Kelia became a Christian disciple, and when the class ended, Kelia was baptized and joined the church. Through the Bible and in a United Methodist congregation, Kelia experienced God's grace.

In what ways can you identify God's grace at work in your life? How does the Bible offer you insights about God's grace?

The Bible Today

Today in United Methodist congregations, institutions, and settings all around the world, persons gather around the Bible to be formed into the image of Jesus Christ. In our private devotions, we read Scripture and reflect on its meaning in our daily lives. We gather in classrooms and living rooms to study the word using resources such as DISCIPLE, *Beginnings*, and various Sunday school studies. At worship, we hear the Bible read and proclaimed, and we respond corporately and individually to its call on our lives. Through hymns and songs, we sing scriptural prayers and teach our children to sing, "Jesus loves me, this I know, for the Bible tells me so." And so it is that we United Methodist Christians discover through the Bible a new and renewed relationship with God and one another.

Over the years, United Methodists have remained open to hearing through the reading of Scripture a fresh word from our living God. While such openness can be frustrating to people who want quick, easy answers, we keep probing for new insights from God. What is more, United Methodists welcome many different perspectives on the biblical text. No one of us has a monopoly on the truth. As Wesley wrote, we "think and let think." In

United Methodist Sunday school classes, at gatherings of laity or clergy, and in many other settings, one can always expect a multitude of passionate opinions all based on the Bible.

How do we live as United Methodist Christians? We begin by following the example of those Bible Moths in Oxford over two hundred and fifty years ago. Pick up a Bible, read it, study it with other Christians, and listen to it in worship. And when we hear God's word, respond. Live as God's living Word calls us to respond. Then we will be like John Wesley and the others who became the people of the Bible.

God of life and hope, lead us as we listen for your word in the Holy Bible. Help us find the comfort of your presence and power. Guide us to renewal and commitment as we respond to your word in our lives. In Christ we pray. Amen.

Notes

1. "The Character of a Methodist," *The Works of Wesley*, vol. 9 (Nashville: Abingdon Press, 1989), pp. 31–46.

2. Albert Outler, ed., *The Works of John Wesley*, vol. 1 (Nashville: Abingdon Press, 1985), p. 105.

3. *The Book of Discipline of The United Methodist Church 2008* (Nashville: The United Methodist Publishing House, 2008), ¶¶103, 104.

4. Edinburgh, April 25, 1765.

5. *The Book of Discipline 2008,* pp. 78–83.

2. What Do We Share with Other Christians?

United Methodist Christians understand themselves as part of Christ's universal church in the world.

"Christ is just like the human body—a body is a unit and has many parts; and all the parts of the body are one body, even though there are many. We were all baptized by one Spirit into one body."
1 CORINTHIANS 12:12-13

The Body of Christ

United Methodist Christians, while part of a distinct denomination, believe that we belong to the global and diverse living body of Jesus Christ, the great crowd of Christians, which has grown and spread for two thousand years. Our ancestors in the faith are the Christians gathered in Jerusalem on the Day of Pentecost (Acts 2), the faithful believers persecuted throughout the Roman Empire, the members of the ancient councils who crafted our creeds, the Eastern Christians who maintained ancient liturgies, the medieval theologians who shaped Western Christianity, the saints who worked with the poor, the European Protestant reformers, the British Anglicans, and Christians today in millions of congregations north and south of the equator. Each United

27

Methodist follower of Jesus is one with other United Methodists and also one with followers of Jesus of every age and land.

United Methodists identify with the church universal because of John Wesley's own openness to other Christians. In his sermon "Catholic Spirit," by which he referred to the church universal, Wesley pulled a quotation from 2 Kings in which Jehu, the king of Israel, invited Jehonadab, mentioned as the founder of the Rechabites in Jeremiah 35:6-10, to join him in serving God.

> Jehu greeted him, and asked, "Are you as committed to me as I am to you?"
> Jehonadab responded, "Yes, I am."
> "If so," said Jehu, "then give me your hand." (2 Kings 10:15)

Wesley developed this quotation into a sermon about the open spirit among all Christians.

Wesley worked with other Christians for the sake of the kingdom of God. As a scholar, Wesley read the writings of theologians throughout the ages and of theologians in his own day. He appreciated the encouragement of the Moravians during his missionary days in Georgia and traveled to Germany to visit the Moravians at Herrnhut. Wesley followed the advice of George Whitefield, another outstanding English preacher, to take his preaching out of church buildings and into the fields. Although Wesley and Whitefield later had a major theological disagreement, they reconciled and remained friends throughout their lives.

When the Methodist movement crossed the Atlantic to North America, the Methodists initially kept close ties to the Church of England, but increasingly followed Wesley's example of serving alongside other Christians by linking arms with the German Evangelicals and United Brethren. In the early 1800s, Methodists, Baptists, and Presbyterians preached side by side at the outdoor revival services on the western frontier. In the late nineteenth century, these denominations worked together to avoid overlap as they sent missionaries around the world. United

Methodists serve the poor and share the gospel hand in hand with Christians all around the world. We affirm ourselves as part of the body of Christ, the universal church.

> Read 2 Corinthians 12. How does this scripture speak to you about the similarities and differences among Christians?

A Common History

The United Methodist Church shares a common history with many Christian communions all over the world. Like them we recognize our beginnings in what Wesley called "the Primitive Church." The fire of Pentecost still shines in the recognized signature of our denomination—the cross and flame. We stand in agreement with the classic affirmations of the church, the Apostles' Creed and the Nicene Creed, both of which are in *The United Methodist Hymnal*. The Apostles' Creed originated in the ancient questions asked of baptismal candidates. It is a series of biblical affirmations about God, Jesus Christ, and the Holy Spirit. In the official baptismal liturgy for The United Methodist Church, the whole congregation recites the Apostles' Creed at each baptism. Similarly, the Nicene Creed, which reflects the consensus of beliefs by bishops in A.D. 325 and A.D. 381 about God, the Father, the Son, and the Holy Spirit, is still an important part of our Christian tradition. While United Methodist Christians are not required to affirm either of these creeds for membership, these creeds express our theological foundations.

While United Methodists honor the contributions of the Eastern Orthodox churches, we have been shaped primarily by the Western Church. Our teachers include Augustine of northern Africa in the fourth century and Aquinas of Italy in the thirteenth century. We are thankful for Roman Catholic saints such as Benedict who taught us to pray, Francis who showed us how to live, and Mother Teresa who demonstrated selfless service. Our family tree includes all these saints and traditions!

United Methodists have a direct kinship with the Church of England, which was formed out of the Roman Catholic Church in the 1530s by King Henry VIII. This new denomination retained elements of its Roman Catholic heritage, while also aligning with Protestant reformers. The Church of England kept a high view of the sacraments of baptism and Holy Communion, but also read Scripture in English and refused to recognize the authority of the pope in Rome. Like the Roman Catholics, the English observed the Christian Year and daily services of prayer. Like the Protestants, the Church of England welcomed married priests and observed only two sacraments. The Church of England understood itself as a middle way between the Roman Catholic and Protestant traditions.

Throughout his life, Wesley remained a faithful priest within the Church of England. Wesley saw the early Methodists as reformers within the Church of England, as a gathering of serious Christians called to be the muscle of a church that had grown spiritually weak. Following the American Revolution, however, Wesley heard the plea of the Methodists in North America for ordained clergy who could baptize, marry, and share Holy Communion. In response, he sent Thomas Coke and two others to ordain preachers for the new denomination. Our forebears always saw us as part of the great line of faithful Christians throughout the ages.

> How does this brief look at our common history with other Christians offer you insights? Does it challenge you? If so, how?

Shared Beliefs

United Methodist Christians accept most major beliefs of other orthodox Christians. We affirm that we are Christians first, United Methodists second. As a sign of the essential oneness of the church of Jesus Christ, we accept persons baptized in other Christian communions as sisters and brothers in Christ. United Methodists share a number of basic Christian affirmations with other Christians that are described in *The Book of Discipline of The United Methodist Church.*[1]

The Trinity

We believe in the triune God—Father, Son, and Holy Spirit—by which God has revealed God's self to humankind in three distinct but inseparable persons. When United Methodists baptize, we like other Christians do so in the name of the Holy Trinity.

How does one describe the mystery of the Trinity, one God in three persons? Christians acknowledge that our one God is infinite in power, wisdom, justice, goodness, and love. In the final analysis, however, we cannot contain God within our definitions. When Job challenged God to explain the unjust suffering in Job's life, God spoke to Job, asking, "Where were you / when I laid earth's foundations? / Tell me if you know" (Job 38:4). When Job heard God's litany of the wonders of creation, Job confessed, "I have indeed spoken about things I didn't understand" (Job 42:3). Like Job, we admit that God cannot be limited by our theological definitions. At the same time, we believe that the Trinity makes clear our human experience of God's self-revelation to us.

The first person of the Trinity, God the Father and Creator, rings true in our hearts and minds. The psalmist reminds us of the need we have to be connected with the God who created us: "My God! My God! It's you— / I search for you! / My whole being thirsts for you! / My body desires you in a dry and tired land, no water anywhere" (Psalm 63:1). Creation itself reveals our creator God to us. Stand outside on a clear, dark night and look up at the millions of twinkling stars. Remember being delighted by the splendor of a colorful rainbow? God draws us in whenever we experience the wonder of God's creation. The psalmist said it well: "Heaven is declaring God's glory, / the sky is proclaiming his handiwork" (Psalm 19:1).

The second person of the Trinity, Jesus Christ, makes visible God's redeeming love for the world. We believe that he was fully human and fully divine and that he offered himself sacrificially to save us from sin and reconcile us to God. Because God raised Jesus from the dead, we believe that our lives will be resurrected and transformed in this life and in the life to come in God's eternal realm. The four Gospels—Matthew, Mark, Luke, and John—witness to Jesus' life, teaching, death, and resurrection. The other books of the New Testament—Acts, all the Epistles, and Revelation—witness to the power of the risen Christ among early believers. Jesus' resurrection ultimately assures us that following Jesus brings life, not death. Jesus also reveals the full potential of who we can be and become as God's people. His teachings often run counter to the teachings of the world. Society encourages us to be consumers of the world's goods and to seek security in our money, possessions, and social status. In contrast, Jesus says, "All who want to save their lives will lose them. But all who lose their lives because of me and because of the good news will save them" (Mark 8:35). Jesus expects his followers to grow in love and service to God and neighbor.

United Methodist Christians also know God through the activity of the third person of the Trinity, the Holy Spirit. In our personal lives and in the life of the church, the Holy Spirit comforts, sustains, and empowers us. The Spirit also stirs within us a desire to become the people God created us to be, both in communion with God and with all of creation. The practices of the early followers of Jesus in Jerusalem, after they experienced the Holy Spirit on the Day of Pentecost, reveal the person of the Spirit. In Acts we read of the first three thousand Christians: "The believers devoted themselves to the apostles' teaching, to the community, to their shared meals, and to their prayers" (Acts 2:42). Everyone was filled with awe, and many wonders and miraculous signs were done by the apostles. All those believers shared what they had with one another. They sold what they owned and gave freely to those in need. The faith of the Christians was contagious, for "the Lord added daily to the community those who were being saved" (Acts 2:47). Similarly, United Methodists filled with the Holy Spirit read the Bible, share Holy Communion, pray, witness miracles, give generously, and share the good news with others.

What does the Trinity say to you about God? How does the Trinity reveal to you the way God acts in our world as Creator, Savior, and Sustainer?

Christian Community

United Methodists believe that God's redemptive love is active throughout the world within the lives of people from every country and culture. No one is beyond the reach of God's redeeming love. Therefore, we welcome everyone, regardless of race, color, national origin, or economic condition, to attend our services of worship, receive Holy Communion, and be baptized and admitted into membership. Like other Christians, United Methodists believe that God changes us and makes us whole in the context of Christian community. We believe that we are initiated into this community of believers through baptism and that in this community we experience the re-creating and transforming power of the Holy Spirit.

Wesley himself developed his spirituality in a Christian home, within a small group of devoted students, and surrounded by other faithful believers. So also today do United Methodist Christians grow in their love for God and others, as we share fellowship meals, gather together for worship and Holy Communion, and participate in prayer groups and Bible studies. While we certainly experience the presence of God alone in prayer or on a solitary walk on the beach, we grow more fully in our faith with the support and accountability of other Christians. The talents and skills of all followers of Jesus are needed to build the church and transform the world.

> How have you experienced growth and transformation within a Christian community? If you have not been a part of a Christian community, what potential do you see for your growth and love of God and neighbor by becoming a part of the community of faith?

The Reign of God

United Methodists also believe with other Christians that the reign of God is both a present and a future reality. God's reign has arrived already, in that already we are empowered by God's Spirit to become more like Jesus. We see evidence of God's present kingdom when church members share a meal at the homeless shelter, join hands to bring disaster relief, and make room in their congregations for strangers and newcomers. Believing that God's reign is already breaking into our world, United Methodists actively engage in social and political reform and do not shy away from taking positions on controversial social issues. United Methodists know, however, that the reign of God is also a future reality. We share with other Christians the hope that God's redemptive and renewing work will be fulfilled in God's realm at the end of time.

> What evidence do you see of God's reign at work in our world? How might you participate in this work? What hope do you see for God's reign in our future?

The Authority of Scripture

As we discussed in chapter 1, we share with other Christians the belief in the Holy Bible as God's authoritative source for knowledge of God and for God's call to return to right relationship with God and with others. We learn of God's forgiveness and salvation through Jesus Christ. We discover there that God empowers and transforms us as individuals and as communities through the Holy Spirit. We also discover that it is God's grace through faith that saves us and not our own works.

> In what ways is the Holy Bible an authoritative source for your life of faith? How does the Bible inform what you know about God and about the way God relates to us? How might the Bible help you in your desire to grow in love of God and neighbor?

Reform and Renewal

Finally, like other Christians, United Methodists affirm that the church universal and our own denomination are in need of continual reformation and renewal. Like other denominations, United Methodists are always seeking to change for the sake of the present and future reign of God. Wesley and the early Methodists sought to reform the Church of England, and so too do United Methodists today seek to change the institutional church, in order that we might more effectively serve God and others. Reform and renewal often begin at the congregational level.

One congregation with which Sally works noticed its shrinking numbers and realized that for too many years members have been satisfied with the people already there and have lost interest in their neighborhood. Instead of closing the church doors, the remaining church members recommitted themselves to repairing the facilities and practicing hospitality to share God's love once again with their neighbors.

How do you think Christian communities need to be reformed and renewed? What could be done better to express God's call to love and service of God and neighbor? How might you contribute to such renewal?

More Alike than Different

While we have theological and organizational differences with other communions, we always remember that we are more alike than different. We will discuss a few of our most distinctive theological beliefs in chapter 4. Yet in broad strokes, how do we compare to other Christian denominations?

The Roman Catholic Church differs from us in that it has seven sacraments, and the pope in Rome is the final authority. Like the Roman Catholics, we have influential bishops and a global perspective. Like the Eastern Orthodox traditions, United Methodists appreciate the worship of the early church. Our worship, on the other hand, has developed a variety of styles through the ages. We celebrate that United Methodists, in many different countries and in a variety of forums, have ongoing theological dialogue and mission activities with these two great traditions.

United Methodists more clearly belong to the Protestant family of communions. A number of Protestant denominations, including the Baptists, Episcopalians, Lutherans, and Presbyterians, share our belief in the two sacraments of baptism and Holy Communion, salvation by grace through faith, and Scripture as our final authority. Yet there are differences. Baptists, who come out of a European reform movement, emphasize adult baptism by immersion and the independence of local congregations. Episcopal congregations, out of the Church of England's Anglican faith, have a strong loyalty to their *Book of Common Prayer*. In addition, Episcopal congregations hire their own pastors, while our pastors are appointed by bishops. Lutherans, who follow the traditions of the German reformer Martin Luther, focus on salvation by faith and permit local congregations to call their own pastors. Pentecostals share Wesley's enthusiasm for the work of the Holy Spirit, but unlike United Methodists, Pentecostals emphasize practicing the gifts of the Holy Spirit such as speaking in tongues in worship. Finally, Presbyterians, who trace their roots to John Calvin, are governed by lay boards and emphasize God's sovereign plan for all of creation. In spite of differences, United Methodists celebrate our connections with these differing Protestant groups.

Interestingly, a variety of Christian traditions is found within our own congregations. Many people who belong to The United Methodist Church were raised in other Christian denominations. We are a theologically diverse denomination.

Out of which Christian tradition did you come? What's the same? What's different for you?

Living and Serving Together

The United Methodist Church is not the only denomination that had its beginnings in Wesley's revival of the eighteenth century. While theological disagreements and social realities have divided the various Wesleyan groups over the years, United Methodists are grateful for the connections that remain between these denominations and pray that one day we will overcome our sins of racism and organizational differences and become one.

In the United States, the Pan-Methodist Commission was formed to build bridges between the different denominations. Over the years, leaders of The United Methodist Church and five historically African American denominations (The African Methodist Episcopal Church, The African Methodist Episcopal Zion Church, The African Union Methodist Protestant Church, The Christian Methodist Episcopal Church, and The Union American Methodist Episcopal Church) regularly meet in recognition of our common ties to Wesley. On a global level, the World Methodist Council, organized in 1881, is an association of denominations that claim John Wesley as their spiritual forefather. This organization includes member denominations from 130 countries. It coordinates missions, resources, and training for Wesleyans around the world.

Within the wider Christian communion, the National Council of the Churches USA works for ecumenical cooperation among Christians in the United States. The United Methodist Church contributes to its ministries and uses educational resources developed through its Committee on the Uniform Series. Churches Uniting in Christ is an organization of ten denominations that have pledged together to express their unity in Christ and to combat racism. The World Council of Churches, formed in 1948, is a global ecumenical group that expresses a mission of seeking unity, a common witness, and Christian service.

Our commitment to working with other Christians reveals itself in many ways. Because we share our hearts, we readily join hands with our sisters and brothers in Christ. The United Methodist Church has always been one of the most open denominations in regard to joining forces with other Christians for the sake of the kingdom of God.

United Methodists have been at the forefront of ecumenical efforts in mission and outreach both locally and globally. We participate in community Thanksgiving celebrations and Holy Week services. Together with other Christians, we build hospitals, schools, and agricultural cooperatives. Millard Fuller, the founder of Habitat for Humanity, an ecumenical housing ministry, honored The United Methodist Church at our 2000 General Conference for being the most supportive denomination in building homes for the working poor around the world. This model of cooperation is true wherever one finds United Methodists.

Cooperative Christian Ministry in Cabarrus County, North Carolina, had its formational meeting at Central United Methodist Church. This ministry linked area congregations in service to the homeless and hungry in the county. For that reason, Roman Catholics, Presbyterians, Lutherans, Baptists, the Salvation Army, and members from a dozen other denominations gathered in Central United Methodist Church's fellowship hall to plan their cooperative service ministry. In communities throughout the United States, you will find similar organizations with the strong support of United Methodists.

> What potential do you see in cooperation with other Christian churches and ecumenical organizations that include a variety of denominations?

One Body of Christ

Our United Methodist ethos is characterized by our ties to the universal church of Jesus Christ. We proudly say that we are United Methodist, but never in an exclusive way. We began with the Apostle Paul's comparison of the church to a human body, explaining that in the same way that a human body needs eyes, ears, hands, and feet to function well, so too does the church need all of the differently talented and gifted church members to be healthy and whole (1 Corinthians 12). No one Christian or solitary denomination can be the body of Christ in service to the world. No one Christian or denomination understands how best to be the church in today's society. Everyone's help is needed to keep the church growing and serving and making disciples of Jesus Christ. And where Christians are joining hearts and hands together, United Methodists are there.

God of all people, thank you for Jesus Christ, who binds us together in Christian love and service. Help all of us grow in our appreciation of our value and the value of those who are different from us. Remind us that we are all important parts of one body of Christ. Amen.

Note

1. See ¶101 in *The Book of Discipline of The United Methodist Church 2008* (Nashville: The United Methodist Publishing House, 2008), pp. 43–44.

3. What Is Our United Methodist Story?

United Methodist Christians emerged from a movement dedicated to spreading scriptural holiness.

"So then let's also run the race that is laid out in front of us, since we have such a great cloud of witnesses surrounding us. Let's throw off any extra baggage, get rid of the sin that trips us up, and fix our eyes on Jesus, the pioneer and perfecter of our faith."

HEBREWS 12:1-2

United Methodist Witnesses

The history of The United Methodist Church begins with the spiritual journeys of John Wesley (1703–1791) and the many women and men who followed after him. Wesley and the other early Methodists understood themselves as part of the Church of England. They knew themselves to be recipients of God's grace. In their stories, we discover the particular ways they lived out their Christian faith, ways of living that continue to define the faith and practices of United Methodist Christians today.

John Wesley

John Wesley's life spanned most of the eighteenth century. His father, Samuel, was a priest in the Church of England. Samuel cherished the worship of the church, took seriously the pastor's role as scholar, and served a small, rural congregation in Epworth for forty years. Susanna, John's mother, also grew up in a clergy family that valued personal holiness. Thanks to her father's training, Susanna became a teacher of both the Bible and spiritual disciplines in her family and local community. Both Samuel and Susanna were serious Christians, who shared a deep love for God and for the Church of England.

Susanna, who taught Bible studies in her kitchen, instilled in John an understanding that women, like men, are gifted for Christian leadership. Even though women were prohibited from most official church offices, Susanna nevertheless found ways to lead. When John questioned the role of women among the early Methodists, his mother reminded him that she had provided the primary spiritual leadership in her husband's parish during one of his absences. Through her influence, women increasingly played a crucial role as class leaders and preachers in the Methodist movement. Barbara Heck, called "the mother of Methodism in the New World," helped establish the first Methodist class in New York City.

Susanna gave birth to nineteen children, ten of whom survived to adulthood. John was Samuel and Susanna's fifteenth child. He was born in 1703. Charles, our great hymn writer, was born in 1707. Susanna insisted that the children attend family devotions at dawn, take seriously their academic studies, and pray the Lord's Prayer as soon as they could speak. The Bible was the textbook by which her children learned to read. Young John's intellect and piety caught Susanna's attention, and she knew God had great work in store for him. At age eleven, John received a scholarship to attend a private boys' school in London, where he excelled academically. Even as a youth, John read the Scriptures daily, observed the daily prayers of the Church of England, and attended worship faithfully.

At age seventeen, John received a scholarship to Oxford University, where he trained for the ministry and was ordained as a priest in the Church of England. Over the years, John sought to reform the Church of England from within. For two years, John served as his father's associate pastor at Epworth. But at age twenty-two, John decided that he was a better teacher than a preacher and moved back to Oxford to teach Hebrew and Greek. Although he was small in size, John became a powerful force, initially in an Oxford Bible study and later in all of English society.

How do you think Wesley's parents and family life contributed to his role as the leader of the Methodist movement? How do you see the role of your family and upbringing in your faith journey?

The Beginning of the Methodists

At Oxford in 1729, Charles invited John to lead a Bible study for himself and two friends. This Oxford Holy Club became the genesis of the Methodist revival. While few people at Oxford took Christianity seriously, the young men in this Bible study did. They read Scripture daily in Greek and Hebrew, prayed often, fasted twice a week, visited the local prison, lived modestly, received Holy Communion weekly, and gave money to the poor. Because of the students' methodical Christian practices, other members of the community labeled them as "Methodists." The students met on Thursday nights, the same night of the week on which it is believed John as a child had joined his mother, Susanna, for a private hour of devotions.

Their disciplined Christianity stood in contrast to the rapidly changing English culture of the eighteenth century. The Enlightenment fostered religious skepticism. The Industrial Revolution transformed English society from a farming culture with extended families nearby to urban, industrialized centers built around coal mines and factories. In the new English society, widespread alcoholism blunted the pain of life, families fell apart, children worked from an early age, and most persons could not read. Public sanitation was nonexistent, and the plague and smallpox spread without effective treatment. The slave trade supported the country's export economy, while persons were imprisoned regularly for nonpayment of debts. The vast gulf between rich and poor extended to the church, where many clergy and landed laity worshiped with their eyes closed to the social crises all around.

Both John and Charles, faithful to their ordination as priests and soon after the death of their father, enlisted in 1735 as missionaries to the colony in Savannah, Georgia. They sought to share traditional Anglican practices with the colonists, many of whom had never been in worship, and with Native Americans and African slaves. On Sundays, John required everyone to attend worship three times, with the first service beginning at 5:00 a.m. The brothers were spectacularly unsuccessful in their efforts and quickly returned to England, both unsure of their faith and their future.

> How do you see the relationship between Christian faith and the surrounding culture?

Aldersgate

Back in England, John despaired of his failures as a follower of Jesus Christ. He doubted his own faith and lacked assurance of his relationship with Jesus Christ. While in Georgia and upon his return to England, a sect of pious Germans called Moravians impressed John with their faith and urged him to find a personal relationship with God. At age thirty-five, in London, John experienced assurance of his salvation. John described his experience in 1738 this way:

> In the evening I went very unwillingly to a society in Aldersgate Street, where one was reading Luther's Preface to the Epistle to the Romans. About a quarter before nine, while he was describing the change which God works in the heart through faith in Christ, I felt my heart strangely warmed. I felt I did trust in Christ, Christ alone for salvation, and an assurance was given me that he had taken away *my* sins, even *mine*, and saved *me* from the law of sin and death.[1]

Have you had a warm-heart experience? If so, what was it like?

The Revival Begins

For the next fifty-three years, John shared his revived faith with anyone who would listen. He spoke at Oxford chapels, in rural congregations, and in living rooms. The year following his Aldersgate experience, George Whitefield invited John to preach outdoors to coal miners and factory workers. John was soon preaching in barns, abandoned factories, and even on top of his father's tomb. His favorite time of day to preach was 5:00 a.m., before laborers began their workday. Thousands came to hear Wesley preach, and the results were immediate. His message connected especially with craftsmen, soldiers, miners, and small farmers. Some people responded to John's preaching with outbursts of prayer, crying, and seizures.

Many leaders within the established church felt threatened by the Wesleyan revival and John's call to personal and social holiness. Preaching outdoors, dynamic hymn-singing, celebrating Holy Communion among the masses, and challenging the reigning religious ethos of eighteenth-century England created great controversy. As the revival grew, many pastors refused to let John preach in their churches, and crowds were often hostile when he preached outdoors. Yet this God-movement grew. With tens of thousands of followers, the movement gained credibility and became the major religious movement of eighteenth-century England. United Methodists today know the dangers of being an established and wealthy denomination. At our best, however, we share the gospel with everyone, including persons and communities often overlooked.

Singing became a key characteristic of the Methodist revival. John's brother Charles was a brilliant and prolific poet, writing almost nine thousand religious poems, which he often set to popular and easily sung music. Many Christians learned the Christian faith by singing Charles's hymns. When Central United Methodist Church in Concord, North Carolina, was established in 1837, the town leaders refused to allow the Methodist sanctuary to be built within the city limits because "the Methodists sang too loud." Later, Fanny Crosby, a blind Methodist musician, wrote gospel hymns like "Blessed Assurance," and today wonderful musicians abound in our denomination. Lively singing still characterizes our worship.

John Wesley was a brilliant organizer. He urged people wanting to grow in their faith to join a small group for a weekly meeting of faith development. Building on his earlier experiences in Oxford, Wesley established thousands of classes around the country. Wesley recruited lay preachers to watch over the groups and often rotated these leaders among the classes in hundreds of cities, towns, and villages. Sunday school classes, DISCIPLE Bible classes, Covenant Discipleship Groups, and other small groups for Christian formation are heirs of this tradition.

Wesley also believed that true commitment to Jesus includes commitment to serving others. He established an orphanage and Sunday schools, a free medical dispensary, a credit union with micro-loans, food pantries, and clothes closets. He empowered women as leaders. Methodists discovered their own leadership skills and became community leaders.

During his lifetime, John Wesley traveled 250,000 miles on horseback and preached over 40,000 sermons. He lived on the salary of a public school teacher and gave away the vast fortune he earned as an author. When Wesley died at eighty-seven, he left behind over 500 preachers, almost 80,000 Methodists in England, 57,000 in the United States, and clusters of Methodists in a dozen other countries around the world to carry on his work.[2] By the end of Wesley's life, Methodism had become a respected and honored segment of English society.

How does the early Methodist movement inspire you or challenge you? What particularly strikes you about the movement and about Wesley's leadership?

The Movement Spreads to America

As Methodists immigrated to the New World, laywomen and men established Methodist classes up and down the eastern seaboard. In 1769, John sent a few lay preachers to strengthen the Methodist societies, and in 1771, a young lay preacher named Francis Asbury joined the work. The Methodists gathered in homes for Bible study, prayer, singing, fasting, and service, even as they continued to be baptized and served Holy Communion by priests of the Church of England.

When the American colonies declared their independence from England in 1776, the Anglican priests left America, leaving the people with little access to the sacraments. In 1784, Wesley sent Thomas Coke, Richard Whatcoat, and Thomas Vasey to North America to consecrate Francis Asbury as bishop and to ordain preachers or "elders" who could administer the sacraments. Wesley also sent documents. One of them was a book of ritual based on *The Book of Common Prayer* (which he renamed *The Sunday Service of the Methodists in North America*) that contained an abridged set of twenty-four Articles of Religion. Another major document was the *Discipline*, which provided the rules by which the American Methodists would function. The Christmas Conference at Lovely Lane Chapel elected and then ordained Coke and Asbury as bishops and preachers who could administer the sacraments. The conference accepted the documents sent to them, and The Methodist Episcopal Church in America was born.[3] Each year the bishops gathered the Methodist preachers and together they wrote rules for their work (*The Discipline*) and published their hymnals and other resources. The Methodists in North America now charted their own course.

Francis Asbury fundamentally shaped the Methodist movement in North America. Born in England, Asbury as a youth joined the Wesleyan revival and became a traveling preacher among the Methodist classes. In 1771, Asbury traveled to North America at Wesley's direction. Asbury never left. When most clergy hid during the Revolution, Asbury remained active. He never married; the new denomination was his passion. Over his ministry of forty-five years, Asbury traveled throughout the eastern states, covering 270,000 miles. He ordained more than 4,000 clergy and preached more than 16,000 sermons. Asbury's focus on disciplined piety, small-group ministry, evangelism, traveling preachers, and the strong role of the bishop profoundly shaped our United Methodist tradition.

Like John Wesley before him, Asbury was committed to our unique practice of itineracy. Both leaders believed in sending passionate preachers where they were needed, without regard to location, salary, or family. In the early days of Methodism, the circuit riders served large geographical regions for six months at a time. In 1776, all of North Carolina was served by three circuit riders. After the American Civil War, when clergy began to marry and to be more educated, it became customary for pastors to locate for one year at a time. Over time, the length of appointments by bishops increased, but still today every United Methodist pastor serves in an appointment made by a bishop.

Important traces of the early tradition of circuit riders remain today. Pastors belong to an annual conference, not a local church, and agree to serve not only a local congregation, but the wider community as well. Bishops regularly review the appointments of clergy and make assignments in the best interest of the whole denomination. Traveling preachers pledge to go where the bishop sends them and to serve the world as their parish.

During the time that The Methodist Episcopal Church was being established, two other groups very similar to the Methodists were forming among German-speaking people in the United States. Philip Otterbein, a German Reformed pastor, and Martin Boehm, a Mennonite preacher who had read Wesley's sermons, both preached an evangelistic message with an emphasis on personal holiness. At the Methodists' Christmas Conference in 1784, Otterbein participated in the ordination of Asbury. Otterbein and Boehm together founded in 1800 the Church of the United Brethren in Christ, which primarily evangelized the German immigrants in the middle Atlantic states. Meanwhile, Jacob Albright, a Lutheran farmer who had listened to Methodist preachers and participated in Methodist classes, created in 1803 the group that would become known as The Evangelical Association. After many twists and turns, all of these denominations joined together in 1968 to create The United Methodist Church.

How does the story of Methodism in America inspire you or challenge you? What particularly strikes you about the formation of The Methodist Episcopal Church in America and about the leadership of Francis Asbury, Philip Otterbein, Martin Boehm, and Jacob Albright?

The Growth of Methodism

The first decades of the nineteenth century saw dramatic growth in our movement. As the nation grew, the Methodists in the United States sent out more circuit riders to the frontier settlers. Instead of waiting for people to establish a congregation and call a preacher, young men rode from settlement to solitary house to town in order to preach, teach, baptize, celebrate Holy Communion, and organize the people in small groups to watch over one another. Most of these preachers owned only the horse they rode, the clothes on their backs, and the books in their bags. Due to the harsh lifestyle, many of these young pastors lasted only a few years in ministry. Thanks to these traveling preachers, one-half of all members of all churches in the United States in 1850 were Methodist.[4]

The Methodists' missionary zeal was extended throughout the United States and beyond to countries around the world. By 1825, Methodists had traveled to Australia, Haiti, South Africa, and Tonga. When the Methodists in North America saw the needs of African Americans and Native Americans, they initiated new ministries. The Methodists in the United States began churches in Korea at the beginning of the twentieth century, and today the independent Korean Methodist Church is starting its own new churches throughout Southeast Asia and even in Afghanistan. United Methodists are now present in over 120 countries and are committed to sharing with people everywhere the saving and transforming power of Jesus Christ.[5]

How do you respond to the work of the circuit riders? to the missionary zeal of early Methodism?

Division

While the Methodist movement grew greatly in the early 1800s, these years also mark the darkest chapters in Methodist history. Divisions occurred, not over theology or doctrine, but around slavery and the authority of clergy. At the originating Christmas Conference of 1784, Richard Allen, an African American preacher, was present and active. Unfortunately, in response to the racism within the church, Allen left the denomination in 1787 and organized in 1816 a group that would become The African Methodist Episcopal Church. Another group of African Americans formed The African Methodist Episcopal Zion Church in 1820. In 1828, in order to establish stronger leadership roles for laity, another group left the denomination and in 1830 began The Methodist Protestant Church.

Another dark chapter in the life of our denomination occurred before the American Civil War. Despite John Wesley's abhorrence of slavery and early efforts to abolish slavery throughout the British Empire, the issue of slavery divided the American denomination. In 1843, the Wesleyan Church split away when the larger denomination refused to support the abolition of slavery.

In 1845, The Methodist Episcopal Church, South separated itself from the northern Methodists, and the two groups remained divided until they reunited in 1939.

Our denomination seeks to heal the divisions based on race that remain among us and is committed to inclusivity. Attempts are made to include diverse representation at every level of church organization. In accordance with our history at its best, women, youth, young adults, and persons from every ethnic group are chosen today as leaders. Our hymnals and books of worship are published in many different languages, including Spanish, French, Tongan, Hmong, German, and Russian, and contain distinctive contributions from each culture. When United Methodists gather today to discuss a topic or form a committee we always ask, "Who is missing from the table?"

> How do you respond to the differences and divisions within Methodism due to racism? What do you think we can learn from these parts of our history?

A Time of Growth

After the Civil War, the Methodists, along with their parallel bodies, grew dramatically. From 1865 to 1913, the membership increased 400 percent.[6] During the Gilded Age, United Methodists trained clergy in new theological schools, formed thousands of new congregations, built great sanctuaries from coast to coast, constructed hospitals, and grew missions throughout the United States and around the world. During these years, a Methodist pastor began Goodwill Industries for the training of the unemployed. The Methodists, Evangelicals, and United Brethren created schools and colleges. A few of the schools include Albright College, Boston University, Duke, Emory, Otterbein, Southern Methodist University, and many others in the United States and other countries. Women led missionary efforts to offer Christ both near and far. The churches expanded their ministries among Hispanics, Native Americans, Asian Americans, and African Americans. Methodists addressed social issues such as child labor, workers' unions, and minimum wage laws.

The heirs of the Wesleyan revival also engaged in many theological debates. Persons formerly associated with the Methodists split to create the Salvation Army, with its focus on social holiness, as well as the Holiness and Pentecostal denominations, with their emphases on personal holiness and a more ecstatic style of worship. Other church debates highlighted the Social Gospel, the place of religion in political affairs, and the role of Scripture in determining theology. The Methodists led the Prohibition movement against alcohol in the nineteenth and early twentieth centuries. Dr. Thomas Bramwell Welch, a Methodist, created "Methodist Unfermented Communion Wine." Frances Willard was a strong leader in the Woman's Christian Temperance Union. Throughout this era, Methodists, Evangelicals, and United Brethren were faithful to their roots and strove always to link vital piety and social witness.

Union and Renewal

Several of these denominations successfully united in the twentieth century. In 1939, the Methodists in the North and South and The Methodist Protestant Church joined to become The Methodist Church. The union of The Evangelical Church and The United Brethren Church in 1946 created The Evangelical United Brethren Church. In 1968, The Evangelical United Brethren Church and The Methodist Church joined to form The United Methodist Church. The red in our cross and flame logo has two flames, indicating the union of these two communions.

Since 1968, The United Methodist Church has seen gains and

failures. Our worldwide vision is broader and more inclusive than ever before. The role of youth, young adults, laity, women, and many racial and ethnic communities is fully established. In the United States and Europe, however, our membership and influence have declined. Some attribute the losses to lack of evangelical zeal, while others blame retreat from controversial social issues. Many United Methodists today are eager to reclaim our emphases on both social and personal holiness. We give thanks that our membership and influence have grown dramatically throughout Southeast Asia and Africa. Within the next ten years, over half of all United Methodists will live outside the United States.

This growth and change reflect the heritage of United Methodists to bend or break the rules for the sake of the church's witness to Jesus Christ. Wesley changed the liturgical practices of the Church of England in order to reach more people. The circuit riders pushed Methodism to the frontier. Women organized the Woman's Foreign Missionary Society to address the health needs of women in India. When the Iron Curtain fell in Eastern Europe, United Methodists established congregations in Moscow, Warsaw, and Macedonia. When we saw a need in Africa for teachers, farmers, clergy, and medical personnel, United Methodists created a great university for the entire continent. Our story continues.

Our United Methodist story has not yet been fully written. John Wesley could never have imagined that the ministry begun with the Bible Moths of Oxford would touch millions of people. As United Methodist Christians today, our heritage calls us to share the gospel even more widely, invite more people into a relationship with Jesus Christ, challenge more boldly the forces of evil in our world, and let the Holy Spirit burn in us ever more brightly, so that the whole world will be drawn to and renewed by Jesus Christ.

Holy God, guide us as we consider how this story of commitment and dedication to scriptural holiness might lead to renewal and growth within our own lives and within the church. In Christ we pray. Amen.

Notes

1. *The Works of John Wesley: Journal and Diaries,* vol. 18 (Nashville: Abingdon Press, 1988), pp. 249–50.

2. Charles A. Sauer, *A Pocket Story of John Wesley* (Nashville: Tidings, 1967), pp. 102–103.

3. Emory Stevens Bucke, ed., *The History of American Methodism,* vol. 1 (New York: Abingdon Press, 1964), pp. 9, 216–17, 223, 226.

4. U.S. Dept. of Commerce, Historical Statistics (1975), p. 392.

5. UMCOM, *The United Methodist Church* (2009), pp. 14–15.

6. U.S. Dept. of Commerce, Historical Statistics (1975), p. 392.

4. What Do United Methodists Believe?

United Methodist emphasize the Christian belief that God's grace—the undeserved, unmerited, and loving action of God—permeates our lives.

"While he was still a long way off, his father saw him and was moved with compassion. His father ran to him, hugged him, and kissed him. Then his son said, 'Father, I have sinned against heaven and against you. I no longer deserve to be called your son.' But the father said to his servants, 'Quickly, bring out the best robe and put it on him! Put a ring on his finger and sandals on his feet! Fetch the fattened calf and slaughter it. We must celebrate with feasting because this son of mine was dead and has come back to life! He was lost and is found!' And they began to celebrate."

LUKE 15:20-24

Practical Divinity

John Wesley's theological practice was to respond to real issues and to focus on how God changes lives. Andy's father, Thomas Langford, once described Wesley's theology as "practical divinity." Like the Apostle Paul, Wesley promoted preaching the gospel, serving the world, and organizing Christians for spiritual growth. "Theology...was to be preached, sung, and lived."[1]

Wesley's practical divinity demanded much of Christians but left room for diversity of theological thought. Wesley explained what was expected of Methodists in his pamphlet "The Character of a Methodist":[2]

> 1. The distinguishing marks of a Methodist are not his opinions of any sort.... But as to all opinions which do not strike at the root of Christianity, we "think and let think."...
> 2. ... We do not place our religion, or any part of it, in being attached to any peculiar mode of speaking....
> 3. Nor do we desire to be distinguished by actions....
> 4. ... By salvation he means holiness of heart and life....
> 5. "What then is the mark? Who is a Methodist...?" I answer: A Methodist is one who has "the love of God shed abroad in his heart...;" one who "loves the Lord his God with all his heart, and with all his soul, and with all his mind, and with all his strength."...
> 17. These are the marks of a true Methodist.... If any man say, "Why, these are only the common fundamental principles of Christianity"... this is the very truth; I know they are no other!

United Methodists today seek this same "character." We want to practice our faith and tell others how God changes lives. Not surprisingly, United Methodists do not agree on all aspects of doctrine. If you put two or three United Methodists together, just as many opinions will surface. We agree on the basics of Christianity, expect moral behavior, share our faith with others, and serve the world; but we do not demand allegiance to a detailed set of beliefs or creedal statements.

How do you respond to these excerpts from "The Character of a Methodist"? What appeals to you? What challenges you?

United Methodist Emphasis on Grace

In spite of our theological diversity, several theological themes define our United Methodist ethos. None of these perspectives are unique to us, but our emphases upon them are distinctive.

The primacy of God's grace stands as our core theological affirmation. Thomas Langford describes grace as God's "redeeming activity of divine love. . . . God's active and continuous presence . . . [that] creates, redeems, sustains, sanctifies, and glorifies."[3] We see God's grace revealed throughout the Bible, especially in the life, death, and resurrection of Jesus Christ.

In *The Book of Discipline*, United Methodists describe the experience of grace as follows: prevenient grace, justifying grace, and sanctifying grace. Prevenient grace affirms that God's grace "comes before" any awareness on our part that God works in the midst of our brokenness.[4] It reveals to us our sin and enables us to respond to God's call to seek God's forgiveness. Justifying grace brings us into a right relationship with God and assures us that we are beloved children of the Almighty. Sanctifying grace helps us grow as Christian disciples and leads us to a life in perfect harmony with God and others.

> How do you respond to Thomas Langford's definition of God's grace? Where have you experienced God's grace at work in your life?

The Journey of Salvation

What does it mean to be saved? For some Christians, salvation depends on receiving the sacraments of the church. For other Christians, salvation comes when one makes a public profession of faith. For still other Christians, the way of salvation involves receiving the gifts of the Holy Spirit and speaking in tongues. We believe that all of these experiences of grace are real, yet none of them alone is sufficient to encompass the whole of God's love for us.

For United Methodist Christians, the word *salvation* means that we are in an intimate relationship with God, who works throughout our lives to make us whole. As Wesley wrote, "by salvation [they mean] holiness of heart and life."

Reflecting on Jesus' parable of the runaway or prodigal son, the way of salvation can be described as a journey on a path with numerous twists and turns. Throughout this journey, we have the freedom to stop, get off the road, or head back from where we came. All of us are on this lifelong journey, but no two people take the same steps in the same sequence.

In this journey of salvation, United Methodists observe that there are a number of distinct moments: God calls us, we listen, and we ask for forgiveness; God embraces us, and we trust; and God empowers us to live faithfully. Each of these distinct moments within the United Methodist understanding of salvation is present in Jesus' parable of the runaway son.

When someone asks, "Are you saved?" how do you respond?

Prevenient Grace

Our salvation journey begins before we are even aware that God is seeking us. Prevenient grace means that God's love comes before we do anything to deserve it. All humans exhibit a self-centeredness that fundamentally severs our relationship with God; we call this condition sin. Yet, despite our failures, God gives us the capacity to sense the underlying presence of God in our lives. God's love surrounds us and prompts our first response to draw near to God.

We see prevenient grace in Jesus' story about the runaway son (Luke 15:11-24). From the moment of the son's birth and long before the son could reciprocate, the father loved his son. The father willingly gave his son freedom to make his own decisions, even when the son demanded his inheritance early. And so God loves us long before we ever love God. Even when we are too busy or distracted to hear, God keeps on speaking to us.

God may speak to us at the beginning of our salvation journey in an everyday conversation or when our conscience prompts us to act. We may hear God whispering to us, while we pray or read the Bible, or God calling to us, when we reflect on a sermon or receive Holy Communion. At significant moments in our lives—when we begin a new job, get married, or have our first child—we often sense God's presence with us. When our world seems to be falling apart—a child dies, a relationship ends, or financial security is lost—we experience God drawing us close. God's prevenient grace is present every moment of our lives. When United Methodists baptize an infant, we do so with assurance that God is already claiming the infant as a member of the household of God. Our only response to this quiet, persistent love is to say, "Thank you, God." The way of salvation, as United Methodists understand it, has begun.

God's prevenient grace prompts "our first glimmer of understanding concerning God's will" and reveals to us that we have failed and need God's forgiveness.[5] Hungry and alone, the younger son lamented his ruined life. Unable to make things better on his own, the son began his journey home. When the younger son understood how badly he had failed, he said, "I'm sorry." In the same way, our recognition of our own failures is evidence of God's grace at work in our lives. When we are truly honest, all of us know that we are not the people God created us to be. All along our spiritual journey, there are moments when

God causes us to become discontent with our lives as they are. Perhaps we question our achievements and values or wonder why we engage in activities that do not bring us fulfillment. Maybe we are overly concerned with our jobs, our possessions, or our families. Whenever we confess that our lives are self-centered, whenever we notice how far we have traveled down the wrong path, God's grace opens our eyes to see our failures, experience God's gift of forgiveness, and find our way home.

How have you experienced God's prevenient grace?

Justifying Grace

Even as God convinces us that we are heading in the wrong direction, God gives us the freedom to choose how to respond. We have the God-given capacity to say yes or no to God. And at the moment we say yes, God forgives our sins, pardons our offenses, and restores us to God's favor. God's justifying grace occurs when God forgives us and assures us of God's love for us. Even as we turn away from our failures and turn toward God, God embraces us and draws us back into a loving relationship with God. God's justifying grace may be appropriated over a lifetime or in a single dramatic moment, but whenever we run toward God, we are welcomed and restored to God's kingdom.

When the runaway son was still some distance from home, his father, who had watched constantly for his son's return, saw him and rushed to embrace him. Even as the son begged for forgiveness, the father was planning a welcome-home feast. At this stage in our salvation journey, we say to Jesus, "Redirect me." And God empowers us to follow Jesus, even as we trust along the way that God's loving protection will never fail.

Some people speak of this one moment of reorientation toward God as conversion. United Methodists speak of conversion as more of a process. Our conversion may be sudden and dramatic or gradual and cumulative. Some people journey toward God from the moment of their baptism as an infant or a child, while other people become Christians through a significant experience as youth or adults. This change in a person's life marks a new beginning, yet it also takes a whole lifetime to unfold.

Have you experienced justifying grace? If so, what was it like? sudden? gradual? a one-time event? a lifetime of growth?

Sanctifying Grace

Sanctifying grace is God's ongoing work in our lives to make us whole and perfect in our love for God and our neighbor. We can only speculate about sanctifying grace in the life of the younger son. We do not know what happened after the father welcomed him home. Did the son remain faithful, working each day in the fields? Did he repay the money he had squandered? We do not know, but because of the father's steadfast love, we suspect that the son's life was changed for the better.

We do know how sanctifying grace affected John Wesley after his heart-warming experience at Aldersgate. Wesley never relied on that one experience, saying complacently, "I have been saved, and nothing more is expected of me." Instead, Wesley sought continually to become more holy in his personal piety and involvement in society. Similarly, United Methodists do not stop their journey of salvation with any one experience. Through prayer, worship, and Bible study, we continue to grow closer to

God. Through our mission outreach to people in need in our communities and around the world, we continue to grow more loving. Throughout our lives, we are nurtured in the church and empowered by God to become the loving people God created us to be. The classic language of sanctification reminds us that the Holy Spirit works within us until we become perfect in love.

Having heard God's call and answered with our repentance, having been embraced by God and having trusted, we are undergirded by God's strength and encouraged to grow. Jesus invites us to be lifelong followers. Through God's sanctifying grace, we respond over and over again to Jesus, "Re-form me. Re-shape me. Make me like you."

> When have you experienced the strength and empowerment of God's sanctifying grace?

The Variety of Salvation Journeys

This lifelong journey with Jesus through all these grace-full moments is what United Methodists mean by salvation. We know Jesus in our hearts and heads, and we serve Jesus with our lips, hands, and feet. Jesus loves us before we love him, and then he offers us forgiveness, assurance, and a holy life. All that Jesus requires of us is a willingness to listen, to kneel, to trust, and to serve.

Every United Methodist Christian participates in this grace-full relationship with Jesus in a different way. No two journeys with Jesus are the same. Our turning to God may be dramatic or quiet, emotional or intellectual, instantaneous or gradual, or a combination of all the above. What is common in all these redirections, however, is that each life-changing experience is initiated by God, who engages each of us as individuals and allows for our own individual response. At every moment, we each must listen for the voice of God over and over again and decide time after time to follow Jesus.

> How do you describe your journey with Jesus?

An Emphasis on Telling the Good News

Because we know this story of salvation, United Methodist Christians are an evangelistic people. Once we understand that we are on a journey empowered by God's grace, we eagerly invite other people to share the journey with us. God's salvation is not our private property. Instead, once we have experienced God's grace, we joyfully share the good news of God's love with others. Wesley was passionate about sharing his experience of God's grace. The Methodists who traveled to the United States; the Germans who immigrated to the New World; the circuit riders who rode on the frontier; and the missionaries who traveled to Africa, South America, and Asia were all committed to telling others about God's grace. Today United Methodists all over the world continue to witness to God's grace in their lives. New faith communities continue to emerge because of our ongoing passion to invite others to experience the fullness of God's grace.

> Have you ever shared your faith journey with someone else? How? Was sharing difficult or easy for you? Why?

Faith and Good Works

United Methodists hold in healthy tension the values of faith and works. We emphasize the importance of faith or a personal relationship with Jesus Christ. At the same time, we preach that our love for God is made real through good works. The dual emphasis of faith and good works is entirely consistent with the journey of salvation we just discussed. In both faith and good works, we discover God's grace at work through us. While faith is essential for a meaningful relationship with God, our relationship with God also takes shape through our care for people, the community, and creation itself. When United Methodist go on mission trips to the Appalachians, the desert Southwest, or Latin America, we both tell our faith stories and build social service centers. Strong faith cannot be separated from good works in the world. When United Methodists hear the voice of God, are forgiven and made right with God, gain the assurance that we are God's children, and grow in our love for God and others, we show to the world both our faith and our concrete actions of service.

How do you see connections between faith and good works in your life? in the church?

Arminians and Calvinists

Our United Methodist way of salvation, our evangelistic outreach, and our dual emphasis upon faith and good works stand in contrast to the teachings of some other Christian communions. Wesley and the theologians who followed him engaged in their most serious debate with theologians attuned to the reformer John Calvin. As we briefly explore the differences between these two theological traditions, we understand more about the heart of our unique United Methodist theology, which is rooted in English Arminian beliefs about grace.

The theological debate was and is between the Reformed traditions, who agree with John Calvin, a sixteenth-century Swiss theologian, and the Methodist tradition, who affirm the beliefs of Jacob Arminius, a sixteenth-century Dutch theologian. Wesley called his own magazine for the early Methodists *The Arminian Magazine.* The discussion revolves around the issue of who can be recipients of God's grace and the role we play in our own salvation. John Wesley dealt with these issues in "The Question, 'What is an Arminian?' Answered by a Lover of Free Grace."

Calvinists and Arminians do agree on most aspects of the Christian faith. Both traditions believe that the result of human sin is complete alienation from God the Creator. Our sin separates us from God so fully that nothing we say or do can reestablish our relationship with God. Calvinists and Arminians both affirm that salvation is a gracious gift of God, which is received through Jesus Christ by faith alone. On these and other issues, the two theological groups believe together.

Yet there are significant differences. Calvinists speak about unconditional election and limited atonement. God's grace through the cross of Jesus Christ comes only to those elected or chosen by an all-knowing God to receive redemption. Calvinists believe in God's destiny for each person and claim that everything happens according to God's plan. For the elected persons, God's grace is irresistible, which means that people chosen by God cannot reject their salvation. Calvinists refer to the perseverance of the saints, which is often interpreted as "once saved always saved." Even if persons turn away from God, their rejection of God is at most temporary. Most Baptists and Presbyterians trace their theological roots to John Calvin.

Arminians describe a more interactive and unfolding relationship between God and humankind. They teach that Jesus Christ died for all people; therefore, God offers free grace to every person. In Arminian terminology, Jesus Christ's atonement on the cross has unlimited power. Instead of speaking about God's irresistible grace, Wesleyans emphasize free will or the God-given human capacity to choose or reject God. Countering the Calvinist argument that humans are too broken to make a decision about God, they say that God's prevenient grace, given to all people, restores human free will and empowers women and men to turn in faith to God. Thanks to God, each person has the capacity and obligation to choose a relationship with God and to follow Jesus. We also have the freedom to reject God's grace or to live holy lives. United Methodists and other Wesleyan denominations trace their theological roots to John Wesley's Arminian views.

What are the practical implications of the theological differences between Calvinists and Arminians? Wesley believed that the coal miners and uneducated industrial workers were people created in the image of God and were recipients of God's grace. Because many of these workers did not attend church and appeared to have no relationship with God, some Calvinists concluded that they had not been chosen by God. Wesley rejected that view and proclaimed that every person had the capacity of living as God's own child. This perspective is why Wesley preached in fields, prisons, and coal mines, encouraging people to choose a transforming relationship with God. Similarly, Asbury did not wait for an established community of elected believers to call someone to preach, but he traveled to the colonies and urged everyone to seek God. The United Methodist emphasis on evangelism proceeds from this view that everyone has the capacity and obligation to accept Jesus Christ as Savior.

Because of his Arminian theology, Wesley urged Methodists in his General Rules "to watch over one another in love, that they may help each other to work out their salvation."[6] United Methodists continue to emphasize the importance of growing in the Christian faith. The teaching "once saved always saved" does not ring true with our United Methodist experience. It is our understanding that followers of Jesus must constantly respond to God's grace at work in their lives and make choices to grow in their love of God and others. Baptism and church membership are not the end goals of life; Christian discipleship demands instead that we continually pray, gather for worship, use our talents, serve the community, and witness to the world to be holy people. Our faithfulness does not save us but reveals instead that the Holy Spirit is at work within us.

One final distinction between Arminians and Calvinists can be summed up in the word *backsliding*. Because the journey of salvation takes a lifetime, Wesley observed that Christians who experienced God's grace could turn their backs on God and walk away from grace. The General Rules provide for removal of members who do not repent and change after reasonable support and encouragement from others in the society.[7] United Methodist congregations today provide persons with opportunities to recommit themselves to Jesus Christ, not once but over and over again. Salvation involves a lifelong commitment to growth in Christian discipleship.

> What do you think of the differences between the Calvinists and the Arminians? What challenges you? What inspires you?

God's Gracious Love

When John Wesley preached his message of God's salvation throughout England, most of the established church leaders found his message strange. Had not God chosen the king, elected the leaders of the nation, and blessed those with power, wealth, and authority? Why did Wesley use his prodigious knowledge and passion to speak to the poor and outcasts? Wesley understood firsthand the gracious love of God. Wesley believed that if he had experienced God's grace, so too could every other child, woman, and man. Wesley was confident that when people heard about God's grace, they would respond, their lives would change, and they in turn would change the world. John Wesley's unique, practical theology remains for United Methodist Christians our most precious heritage.

Loving God, help us become more sensitive to your active grace in our lives. Prompt us to grow as disciples of Jesus Christ and to work out our salvation in response to your saving love. In Christ we pray. Amen.

Notes

1. Thomas A. Langford, *Practical Divinity: Theology in the Wesleyan Tradition* (Nashville: Abingdon Press, 1983), p. 21.

2. "The Character of a Methodist," *The Works of Wesley,* vol. 9 (Nashville: Abingdon Press, 1989), pp. 33–41.

3. Langford, *Practical Divinity,* p. 24.

4. *The Book of Discipline of The United Methodist Church 2008* (Nashville: The United Methodist Publishing House, 2008), pp. 45–47.

5. Ibid., p. 46.

6. Ibid., ¶103, p. 72.

7. Ibid., p. 74.

5. How Do United Methodists Serve God and Neighbor?

United Methodists organize in ways that support a ministry of love and service to God and to one another.

"Then the king will say to those on his right, 'Come, you who will receive good things from my Father. Inherit the kingdom that was prepared for you before the world began. I was hungry and you gave me food to eat. I was thirsty and you gave me a drink. I was a stranger and you welcomed me. I was naked and you gave me clothes to wear. I was sick and you took care of me. I was in prison and you visited me.'

"Then those who are righteous will reply to him, 'Lord, when did we see you hungry and feed you, or thirsty and give you a drink? When did we see you as a stranger and welcome you, or naked and give you clothes to wear? When did we see you sick or in prison and visit you?'

"Then the king will reply to them, 'I assure you that when you have done it for one of the least of these brothers and sisters of mine, you have done it for me.'"

MATTHEW 25:34-40

The Outward Journey

United Methodist Christians balance their personal journeys with Christ with vital works of service to transform the world. Spiritual disciplines, such as worship and prayer, draw us into a closer relationship with Jesus Christ, but these acts of piety are incomplete without accompanying acts of service. Jesus himself healed the sick, fed the hungry, and worked among the poor. If we want to follow Jesus, we are called to do the same. In his parable about the final judgment, Jesus told his disciples that people will be held accountable for the ways in which they served, or did not serve, people in need. On our salvation journey to become whole and loving persons, we have the holy responsibility to give food to the hungry, water to the thirsty, hospitality to the stranger, clothing to the poor, comfort to the sick, and support to the prisoner.

Our United Methodist perspective stands in stark contrast to strong voices in the culture around us today. Many in our modern society believe that everybody must fend for themselves. If we have food, clothing, and shelter, there is no obligation to make certain that other people have those basic needs met, too. As followers of Jesus, however, we are called to live in community and to care for the material and spiritual needs of others. Our vision is that the world will know us, not only by our warm hearts, but also by our willingness to lend a helping hand.

How does Matthew 25:34-40 speak to you about a balance between the inward and outward journeys of faith?

John Stewart and the Wyandot Mission

"The Wyandot Indian Mission" is a lithograph that hangs in Andy's office. The picture depicts the story of John Stewart, an African American freeman who once lived "a drunken and dissolute life." In 1816, Stewart was on his way to the river to end "his worthless existence." En route he overheard a Methodist worship service. Stewart "heard the singing, hesitated, entered the church, and was gloriously converted." Following his conversion, Stewart felt God's call to preach the gospel to the Wyandot Indians in Ohio. He established a mission among the Wyandots by wearing the rough clothing of a freeman, binding his long hair in Wyandot fashion, and preaching about Jesus in the Wyandot language. Stewart's outreach ministry inspired the organization of the Methodist Missionary Society in 1819. When Stewart died in 1823, J. B. Finley, an Anglo circuit rider, continued Stewart's ministry to the Wyandots. The passion of John Stewart to share God's grace with unchurched Native Americans is the same passion that motivates United Methodists to participate in mission efforts all around the world.

> What feelings or thoughts do you have about African American John Stewart's outreach to the Wyandot tribe in 1816? How does the story challenge you or inspire you?

Faith into Action

John Wesley was adamant that the early Methodists put their faith in Jesus into action. The first two General Rules for the Methodists emphasized the importance of becoming more

Christlike in behavior. The rules to "do no harm" and to "do good" continue to set the tone for how United Methodist followers of Jesus serve the world today.[1]

Wesley gave examples of behavior unacceptable for Methodists striving to keep the first rule of "doing no harm, by avoiding evil of every kind." According to Wesley, such evil practices include "taking of the name of God in vain,... drunkenness,... the giving or taking things on usury... doing to others as we would not they should do unto us... the putting on of gold and costly apparel... laying up treasures upon earth."[2] United Methodists are keeping the first rule when they do not speak disrespectfully of God and other people, do not abuse drugs and alcohol, do not engage in business practices that rob from the poor, do not treat others differently than they would want to be treated, do not flaunt material possessions, and do not hoard their wealth.

Wesley's second rule has had an even larger impact on our United Methodist service to the world: "doing good of every possible sort, and as far as is possible, to all [people]: To their bodies... by giving food to the hungry, by clothing the naked, by visiting or helping them that are sick or in prison. To their souls, by instructing, reproving, or exhorting all we have any intercourse with.... By doing good, especially to them that are of the household of faith."[3] We are expected not only to avoid evil; we are called to do what is right.

Significantly, Wesley listed the third rule—"attending upon all the ordinances of God," that is, following the spiritual disciplines of attending worship, receiving the Lord's Supper, praying, reading the Bible, and fasting—only after he instructed the Methodists to focus on their holiness in the world by doing no harm and doing good.[4] In order to be wholly Christian, our spiritual disciplines must lead us to act in ways that bring love and justice to society. The Methodists in England had a dramatic impact on the lives of others when they set up credit unions, established clothing closets and health clinics, and led protests against unfair lending practices and slavery. Their caring spirit grabbed people's attention. Neighbors and coworkers were attracted to the early Methodist Bible studies and worship, in large part because they already knew what the Methodists were about. Similarly, the mission projects of United Methodists today are often the entry points for new followers of Jesus.

> How do you respond to Wesley's General Rules to do no harm, do good, and attend to the ordinances of God? What connections do you see between these rules and the idea of putting faith into action?

Serving the World

In most United Methodist congregations, this ethos of service can be observed as soon as one walks in the front door. One might notice a shopping cart to collect food for the local food pantry, a basket for health kits for a flood-ravaged area, or a sign-up sheet for mission project volunteers. Sally remembers the excitement of church members in the Avery Parish when together they established the Ram's Rack, a food and clothing center that in its first year provided food to almost 10 percent of the rural mountain county. People from the Avery Parish were just as excited when they signed up for the CROP Walk for Hunger and trudged up and down mountain roads on behalf of hungry families on the other side of the world.

> How do you see churches working to serve others, especially people who are poor, sick, hungry, imprisoned, or oppressed? How might you be a part of this work?

Organized for Ministry

The organizational structure of The United Methodist Church enables us to be in ministry to others locally, nationally, and globally. Our connectional system was designed for our mission "to make disciples of Jesus Christ for the transformation of the world." John Wesley once wrote, "I look upon all the world as my parish."[5] So too do United Methodists today. And like Wesley, we know that we can accomplish more for others together than any of us can separately.

Similar to the United States government, The United Methodist Church has three basic branches of government. The General Conference, which gathers every four years for two weeks, serves as the legislative branch of the denomination. Around one thousand lay and clergy delegates write legislation for *The Book of Discipline of The United Methodist Church*, which serves as our official book of doctrine, procedures, and laws. The General Conference continually updates denominational policy and is the only body to speak definitively for the entire denomination. The Judicial Council, which is composed of nine persons, resolves legal differences within the denomination. Although The United Methodist Church does not have a clear administrative branch, the Council of Bishops provides general oversight to the denomination.[6]

United Methodists are community people at their core. In our individualistic, do-it-alone culture, United Methodists emphasize the importance of relationships and partnerships. We share covered dish lunches, engage in work days at the church, prepare funeral meals, receive special offerings, worship together, and serve our neighbors hand in hand. When Andy's congregation completed its last pictorial directory, it also created one large montage that at a distance appears to be the church sanctuary. When you come up close to the picture, you see the individual photographs of everyone in the congregation.

How are we organized beyond the local congregation? Every

local congregation is clustered with neighboring United Methodist churches in regional units called districts. Each district is led by a district superintendent, who is appointed by a bishop to support the pastors and local churches in their mission to make disciples. Often the district churches work together in the community. In the Salisbury District, where Sally is appointed district superintendent, the local churches have partnered in Latino ministries, building projects, new church starts, unemployment response ministry, and ministries with the homeless.

Every district belongs to a larger unit called the annual conference. The Western North Carolina Conference, for example, has fifteen districts. While laypersons are members of local churches, the clergy hold their church membership in an annual conference. Bishops, who have been elected by clergy and laity at regional conferences, are assigned to oversee the work of the clergy and local congregations in each annual conference. The United Methodists in each annual conference join together in ministry and mission outreach. Annual conferences sponsor new congregations, empower local churches to do ministry, provide health care for retired clergy, support United Methodist colleges and retirement homes, build homes for persons with intellectual and developmental disabilities, organize mission teams to serve throughout the world, and the list continues.

On national and global levels, United Methodists have general agencies, councils, and commissions that coordinate and guide our mission to the world. These bodies are led by boards that include bishops, clergy, and laity. Bishops, who each preside over one or more annual conference, also serve as the spiritual and administrative leaders of our whole denomination. The United Methodist Church has no central church headquarters. Instead, the denominational agencies are located in several locations, including Washington, D.C.; New York City; and Nashville. Together the agencies manage our global finances, care for pensions, send forth missionaries, design hymnals, lobby politicians, prepare Bible studies, and advocate for women and persons of color. The denomination as a whole also responds to natural disasters throughout the world, supports thirteen seminaries in the United States and Africa University in Zimbabwe, and contributes to historically Black colleges. The local churches, districts, annual conferences, and general agencies work together, in order that The United Methodist Church may make disciples of Jesus Christ for the transformation of the world.

> How do you see the relationships between structured organization for mission and ministry, the daily life of a Christian believer, and the call of Jesus to attend to the needs of people who are hungry, thirsty, or without adequate shelter and clothing?

The Connection

United Methodists call the relationship between all these units—the local congregation, the district, the annual conference, and the general church—connectionalism. Connectionalism is not an organizational chart but an interactive set of relationships that offers an ongoing dialogue between every part. Pastors and laypeople from local congregations serve on all the boards and agencies of our church, and the boards and agencies assist local congregations in their mission. Everyone is accountable to everybody else. When you join one United Methodist congregation, you become a member of the entire "connection."

Where does the money placed in the offering plate at your local church go within this connectional system? Out of every $1,000 in our offering plates, $845 stays in the local church; $124 goes to jurisdictions, annual conferences, and districts; $22 goes to general apportionments; and $9 goes to other general funds. Expenses and missions beyond the local level are supported through "apportionments," or fair-share askings, which have been equitably allocated to local congregations based on their ability to give.[7]

As we write this resource, our global connection is focusing on four areas of ministry:

- Combating the diseases of poverty by improving health globally.
- Engaging in ministry with the poor.
- Creating new places for new people and revitalizing existing congregations.
- Developing principled Christian leaders for the church and the world.[8]

Through these efforts, United Methodists are educating thousands of new leaders; starting hundreds of new congregations while empowering thousands of existing churches; providing emergency help for the poor while seeking ways to move people out of poverty; and sending money, resources, and people to improve health care worldwide.

Another example of how our connectional system works is seen in the way the denomination holds title to real property. At the local level, for example, the title for the property and the church buildings on it is not held by church members but is held in trust for The United Methodist Church. This means that the resources of each local church are intended for ministry, which extends the mission of the entire connection. The same is true for property at every level of the denomination. Begun by Wesley, this model ensures that each part of our connection perpetuates United Methodist doctrine and practice for the sake of the whole.

Impact Day is a great illustration of how our connectional system works. On June 5, 2010, the entire Western North Carolina

Annual Conference celebrated a Saturday work day to serve our neighbors. The United Methodist General Commission on Communication, one of our general agencies, designed logos, provided promotional advice, and donated seed money. Annual conference staff worked with the general agency on TV and radio promotion and provided Internet and newspaper coverage throughout Western North Carolina. All fifteen districts encouraged members and friends of all 1,200 congregations in the annual conference to participate. On Impact Day itself, over 13,000 United Methodists wearing red T-shirts prepared meals for the homeless, packed emergency kits for flood victims, planted community gardens, served free food in parks, and joined together in hundreds of other projects. United Methodists made a larger impact together than any one of them could have made alone. Energetic volunteers built wheelchair ramps for disabled adults, washed windows at neighborhood schools, and painted walls of Habitat houses. Caring children designed greeting cards for hospital patients and gave hugs to nursing home residents, while youth groups showed up to pull weeds, wash vans, and pick up trash. Meanwhile, praise bands performed in public parks, women crocheted prayer shawls, and gardeners planted vegetables in community gardens. On one day, in one small region of the world, United Methodists came together to make a positive impact on the lives of others.

What insights did you gain about "the connection"? What feelings or thoughts do you have about our work as a connectional church?

The Global Connection

The United Methodist connectional system works globally as well as locally to serve others in the name of Jesus Christ. Thanks to the United Methodist Committee on Relief (UMCOR), for example, United Methodists are among the first to respond quickly when disaster strikes. Because collections for the general church pay administrative costs, UMCOR can use 100 percent of its monies for relief work. Whether it is an earthquake in Haiti, tornadoes in the Midwest, an oil spill in the Gulf of Mexico, or flooding in Pakistan, United Methodists are there to serve. The world is our parish.

Where can you learn more about our connectional system? The basic website for our denomination is www.umc.org. This site is the portal to thousands of other sites that provide information about every aspect of The United Methodist Church.

> If you have a computer and can go online, explore www.umc.org. What do you see? What thoughts, feelings, and insights do you gain about The United Methodist Church from this website?

The Social Principles

For United Methodists, keeping the first two General Rules of doing no harm and doing good has widespread social implications. As followers of Jesus, we believe that it is impossible to put God's love into action without getting involved in the political and social arena. While we share with other Christians basic affirmations of faith such as the Apostles' Creed and the Nicene

Creed, "The United Methodist Social Creed" is uniquely ours. The creed reads:

> We believe in God, Creator of the world; and in Jesus Christ, the Redeemer of creation. We believe in the Holy Spirit, through whom we acknowledge God's gifts, and we repent of our sin in misusing these gifts to idolatrous ends.
>
> We affirm the natural world as God's handiwork and dedicate ourselves to its preservation, enhancement, and faithful use by humankind.
>
> We joyfully receive for ourselves and others the blessings of community, sexuality, marriage, and the family.
>
> We commit ourselves to the rights of men, women, children, youth, young adults, the aging, and people with disabilities; to improvement of the quality of life; and to the rights and dignity of all persons.
>
> We believe in the right and duty of persons to work for the glory of God and the good of themselves and others and in the protection of their welfare in so doing; in the rights to property as a trust from God, collective bargaining, and responsible consumption; and in the elimination of economic and social distress.
>
> We dedicate ourselves to peace throughout the world, to the rule of justice and law among nations, and to individual freedom for all people of the world.
>
> We believe in the present and final triumph of God's Word in human affairs and gladly accept our commission to manifest the life of the gospel in the world. Amen.[9]

While not everyone agrees with every aspect of every clause of our Social Creed, this statement of faith holds before us a vision of the new creation God has called us to make visible and real. Because of our allegiance to these statements of belief, every four years at General Conference we also revise *The Book of Resolutions of The United Methodist Church*, which includes statements about the social concerns approved by General Conference. United Methodists, in the tradition of Jesus Christ of Nazareth, take stands on issues from sex trafficking to global warming to stem-cell research to national health care.

What challenges you or inspires you in the Social Creed?

Serving in a Multireligious World

United Methodists also recognize that we serve God in a world surrounded by persons of many other religious traditions. While many of us may know more about Judaism, Islam, and other ancient religions, every day new sects and ideologies emerge around us. Religious tensions increasingly are exploding in violence and hatred. Much of the world's poverty, oppression, and warfare originate in religious struggles. How do United Methodists respond to the diverse religious cultures around us as we attempt to do no harm and do good? As followers of Jesus, we seek to be both neighbors and witnesses.[10]

First, we honor people who follow other religious traditions as individuals created in the image of God. Jesus reminded the Jews of the inherent value of the Samaritans and shared his blessings with the Syrophoenician woman. Following the example of Jesus, United Methodists must meet, know, respect, and honor others, especially those persons who seem most strange to us. At all times, we are expected to love our neighbors and live in community with them.

Second, United Methodists are called to share our witness that Jesus Christ is our Savior and the Savior of all creation. Through our words and deeds, Jesus asks us to share God's grace and to invite others to follow Jesus with us. We do so with boldness, but also with humility. United Methodists value dialogue with our neighbors. We can learn from them, and they can learn from us. This perspective is why many United Methodist congregations spend time studying other religions and hosting interfaith events, at which different voices may be heard.

Throughout its history, The United Methodist Church has celebrated its mission to be neighbors and witnesses to many different people, including Koreans, Macedonians, Vietnamese, Liberians, Hmong, and Norwegians. Increasingly, and blessedly, United Methodists from those cultures now are coming to the United States to be neighbors and witnesses to a wide variety of American cultures. When a Korean United Methodist pastor is appointed to an Anglo congregation in the United States, blessings can abound for everyone.

Following in the Footsteps of Jesus

This chapter has covered a broad range of issues from individual acts of compassion to global efforts to transform the world. Wesley's instructions to do no harm and to do good are still followed by United Methodists today. As an extension of Jesus' ministry to preach good news to the poor, release to the captives, and recovery of sight to the blind, we followers of Jesus Christ continue to make the whole world our place of ministry.

God of all people and all creation, guide us to honor one another, love another, and serve one another in the name of Christ, who shows us your love, mercy, and justice. We pray in his name. Amen.

Notes

1. *The Book of Discipline of The United Methodist Church 2008* (Nashville: The United Methodist Church, 2008), ¶103, p. 73.

2. Ibid.

3. Ibid.

4. Ibid., p. 74.

5. *Journal,* 11 June 1739, *The Works of John Wesley,* vol. 19 (Nashville: Abingdon Press, 1990), p. 67.

6. *The Book of Discipline 2008*, pp. 23–27, 38, 317.

7. "The United Methodist Church" by UMCOM in 2009, based on July 2008 facts from GCFA, p. 34.

8. See http://www.umc.org/site/c.lwL4KnN1LtH/b.4443111/k.D 720/Four_Areas_of_Ministry_Focus.htm.

9. *The Book of Discipline 2008*, ¶166, pp. 129–30.

10. See "Called to Be Neighbors and Witnesses," *The Book of Resolutions of The United Methodist Church 2008* (Nashville: The United Methodist Publishing House, 2008), pp. 280–89.

6. How Do United Methodists Live and Worship?

United Methodist Christians celebrate God's salvation and grace in Jesus Christ, practice spiritual disciplines, and put Christian belief into daily practice.

I encourage you to live as people worthy of the call you received from God. Conduct yourselves with all humility, gentleness, and patience. Accept each other with love, and make an effort to preserve the unity of the Spirit with the peace that ties you together. You are one body and one spirit just as God also called you in one hope. There is one Lord, one faith, one baptism, and one God and Father of all who is over all, through all, and in all.

EPHESIANS 4:1-6

Inward Piety and Outward Service

United Methodist Christians belong to the church universal but have their own rich history and practical theology. How then do we live, worship, and serve today? To paraphrase Paul, do we lead lives worthy of God's call? United Methodists put their relationship with God into practice through both personal and social holiness. They seek to maintain in their daily lives a balance between faith and works, belief and action, and inward piety and outward service.

When people began to gather around John Wesley to learn how to grow as followers of Jesus Christ, he created small groups for personal growth and mutual accountability. Wesley believed that humans are not born Christian but may be formed into disciples within the right environment and guided by the right instructions. After the beginning of the Methodist movement, he wrote a pamphlet outlining his expectations of the Methodists. Wesley republished "The General Rules" more often than anything else he ever wrote.[1]

In essence, Wesley expected the Methodists to observe three basic practices: do no harm, do good, and observe spiritual disciplines. Wesley believed that these practices would shape Methodists into mature Christians. "The General Rules" may seem quaint and filled with unfamiliar language to some today, but they continue to serve as a foundation for how to live as United Methodist Christians. With God's grace, these rules help us grow in inward and outward holiness as disciples of Jesus.

> What rules do you follow in your life? How might you put Wesley's rules into practice in your daily life?

Classes and Small Groups

The success of the Methodist movement rested on Wesley's practical method of empowering people to help each other become serious disciples of Jesus Christ. In every community, he established small neighborhood groups called "classes." Wesley based these classes on his experiences with the Holy Club, Puritan societies, Moravian bands, and practices of the early church. The typical class consisted of twelve persons, men and women of all ages. They met in members' homes, shops, or schoolrooms for an hour or two each week.

The class leader served as the glue that held each class together. Laymen and -women, chosen on the basis of their spiritual maturity, led the classes. Each class met during the week, and the program for the class began with an opening hymn. The members then read through the three rules, and each person reported on his or her success or lack of success with the rules. In response to the first rule to do no harm, persons might report that they had avoided strong drink or refused to gossip throughout the previous week. When asked if they kept the second rule to do good, members might reply that they had visited the prison or taken food to a hungry neighbor. Finally, in their report on the third rule to keep spiritual disciplines, class members might share that they had attended worship on Sunday and had prayed every day.

While reporting on their success, the members would also tell one another how they had fallen short that week in keeping the three rules. At the end of each class meeting, members prayed with one another, sang a hymn, and departed until meeting together again the next week. As Wesley wrote, such a society is no other than "a company of people having the *form* and seeking the *power* of godliness, united in order to pray together, to receive the word of exhortation, and to watch over one another in love, that they may help each other to work out their salvation."[2]

Today many congregations are discovering anew the power of small groups for Christian formation. While worship brings the congregation together in prayer, praise, and edification, small groups can challenge us on a personal level. Wesley understood the power of balancing large gatherings for worship with small groups for personal accountability and growth.

What is your experience with small groups? How might such groups nurture your life of faith?

Observing Spiritual Disciplines

Methodists are called to practice the spiritual disciplines, which help them grow closer to God. This practice is the third rule, which instructed people to do what God commanded them to do: worship, hear the word proclaimed, receive the Lord's Supper, pray, read the Bible, and fast.[3] Wesley called these disciplines or ordinances of God "means of grace." In his sermon "The Means of Grace," he explained that these religious practices were the channels through which God's grace was usually received. The full riches of God's grace are poured out when Christians gather with others to hear the Scriptures read and interpreted, share the bread and cup of Holy Communion, participate in a service of baptism, offer prayers for themselves and others, observe a fast of one meal or more, and meet in small groups to watch over one another in love.

Followers of Jesus continue to grow in faith through the means of grace described by Wesley. On any given Sunday in any given United Methodist congregation, people listen attentively when the Bible is opened and read in order to hear God speak. Women, men, youth, and children lift to God their joys and concerns and know that God listens. When we watch a child being baptized or kneel around the table for Holy Communion, we sense the presence of Jesus Christ. One holy moment in Andy's congregation occurred when Pastor Reta, who had been diagnosed with cancer, knelt down for the children to lay hands on her for healing. Such holy moments happen regularly in every United Methodist congregation.

How have you experienced the presence and support of God through spiritual disciplines or the "means of grace"?

Worship

Individuals certainly receive God's grace when they pray in private or read their Bibles at home alone. But for Wesley, the spiritual disciplines were also community activities. Following Jesus as United Methodists always includes living our lives connected to others, both in our local congregations and with United Methodists and Christians around the world. Worship is the most visible way that United Methodists stay connected with God and with one another, whether we gather in a small white chapel, a huge stone sanctuary, or the open air.

United Methodists follow a "Basic Pattern of Worship—Entrance, Proclamation and Praise, Thanksgiving and Holy Communion, and Sending Forth"—described in our *United Methodist Hymnal* and *United Methodist Book of Worship*. We gather together, we are attentive to the word of God, we give thanks to God for the gospel and share the Lord's Supper, and then we leave worship to serve the world.

While the basic pattern is constant, a wide variety of styles of worship characterize our local congregations. When the people of God gather, the Spirit moves them to worship in diverse ways, according to the needs of the community. Congregations of different sizes, in different regions, of different racial and ethnic compositions, and with different local traditions worship in varying styles. People gather in a small Appalachian congregation to hear the call through the music of a mandolin, while a megachurch in Dallas hears the same call with a worship band and video projection. Other followers of Jesus congregate in a small chapel and respond to God's call with weekly Communion, while still other United Methodists offer their own response to God in a large gothic sanctuary through organ music and chanted prayer. No two United Methodist congregations worship in the same way, but a basic unity undergirds all our diversity.

At the heart of United Methodist worship is a rhythm of "call and response." This call and response rhythm begins to take shape when musicians call worshipers to respond to the opening music by listening or singing or when the pastor asks for concerns and celebrations of the gathering community. The heart of worship's call is usually in the service of the word or the preaching service: people read and listen to Scripture proclaimed and interpreted. A response follows this call. The response may be a prayer, an offering of financial or material gifts for people in need, or the Lord's Supper or Holy Communion.

This call and response rhythm reflects the experience of two of Jesus' disciples on the road to Emmaus on the first Easter (Luke 24:13-35) and is confirmed by our own worship experiences. When the two disciples fled Jerusalem in confusion over the events of that day, they were joined and comforted by the risen Christ. In much the same way, the risen Christ joins us when we gather for worship, often preoccupied or burdened with the concerns of our lives. Jesus "opened the Scriptures" to the two disciples and caused their hearts to burn. So too do our hearts burn when the Scriptures are read to us, and we respond by praising God. In Emmaus, Jesus took and blessed bread, which he then broke and gave to the two disciples. Similarly, we take, bless, break, and give the bread and cup around the Communion table in the name of the risen Christ. And just as Jesus disappeared and sent the disciples into the world with faith and joy, so too does Jesus send us forth at the close of worship to serve and to share the good news with the world.

When Sally and Andy served seven United Methodist congregations in the mountains of North Carolina, our members decided to send out a mission team to Panama in Central America. Call and response became real. We called our missionaries by preaching during worship about the need to serve our neighbors to the south. We wondered if anyone would respond. At the end of our sermons, however, at least one person from each congregation responded and offered his or her time and energy. We had only expected two or three persons to respond. Now we had a problem. How could we pay the expenses of this mission with so little money budgeted? The individuals who had said yes to the mission trip responded by calling on their United Methodist sisters and brothers. Almost immediately other persons came forward to contribute to the cost; we received more than enough money to pay for the entire trip.

How else do United Methodist Christians worship? We have services of Christian marriage and a service of death and resurrection. Many United Methodist congregations observe the Christian Year: Advent, Christmas, the Day of Epiphany, Ordinary Time, Lent, Easter, the Day of Pentecost, and Ordinary Time again. As we journey through the year with Jesus Christ, we learn to walk in his footsteps. Congregations also celebrate services of healing, blessings of animals, love feasts, morning or evening prayer services, and many other special services to reconnect us with God. The United Methodist revival begun by Wesley continues whenever people gather to hear God's call and respond to the gospel of Jesus Christ.

How do you describe the styles of worship in churches you have attended? What kind of worship most inspires you?

Holy Communion and Baptism

United Methodists practice two sacraments, Holy Communion and baptism. In Holy Communion, also called the Lord's Supper or the Eucharist, we experience through word, sign, and action the living presence of Jesus Christ in our lives. Wesley believed that Holy Communion was the essential act of worship and he received Communion at least once a week and more often when possible. As Jesus took bread and cup, blessed the bread and cup, broke the bread, and gave it to his disciples, so when we share the meal we experience anew the real presence of God. Baptism is both an initiation into the body of Christ and a celebration of God's grace at work in human life.

United Methodists practice open Communion. That means that everyone is invited to Christ's table; there are no restrictions by virtue of a person's age, ability to reason, membership in a local congregation, or even baptism. We welcome the visitor, the stranger, the member, the guest, the saint, the sinner, the old, and the young to the table of Jesus Christ. Our inclusive invitation is open to everyone, because we trust that the prevenient grace of God is already inviting persons to the table. As our invitation to Holy Communion says clearly:

> Christ our Lord invites to his table all who love him,
> who earnestly repent of their sin
> and seek to live in peace with one another.[4]

Like Holy Communion, baptism was initiated by Jesus Christ as a symbol and pledge of God's love for us. The baptismal covenant, again as found in our *United Methodist Hymnal* and *United Methodist Book of Worship*, proclaims our adoption by grace and our response of faith and love. Through baptism, we are incorporated into the church universal. Because baptism initiates us into Christ's universal church, United Methodists recognize all Christian baptisms, such as Sally's baptism by immersion in a Baptist congregation.

United Methodists may baptize by any of the modes used by Christians. Persons have the choice of being baptized by sprinkling, pouring, or immersion. Sally and Andy have baptized in rivers, in borrowed Baptist pools, and beside small fonts. But no matter the mode or location of baptism, the presence of water reveals the rich and diverse symbolism given to baptism by the Bible. Just as water cleanses and quenches thirst, for example, so too does the water of baptism signify the removal of sin and the gift of life eternal in Jesus Christ.

As another sign of God's prevenient grace, United Methodists celebrate the baptism of infants and children, as well as youth and adults. Nowhere does the New Testament record that Christian families delayed the baptism of their children until they could make their own profession of faith. Jesus' words "Allow the children to come to me.... Don't forbid them, because the kingdom of heaven belongs to people like these children" (Matthew 19:14) remind us that our Lord has expressly given to little children a place among the people of God. When Sally and Andy's two daughters were baptized as babies, the family and congregation confessed in faith that God's grace was already at work in their lives.

The salvation journey, of course, does not end with baptism. Infants and children who have been baptized later take the vows of Christian discipleship and full membership in a service of confirmation. In addition, youth and adults who were baptized and joined the church years earlier may reaffirm the baptismal covenant in worship with others. On the first Sunday of the year or at another significant time for the congregation, for example, everyone may be invited to reaffirm their baptismal vows.

Followers of Jesus will have fresh, new experiences of God's presence in their lives. Sometimes the experience is so life-changing that a person asks to be baptized again. United Methodists do not rebaptize. We understand that God's promises to us in our baptism are steadfast. Once baptized, we are initiated into Christ's body the church and are members of the family of God.

What thoughts or feelings do you have about the way United Methodists practice Holy Communion and baptism? How do you connect the practices with God's grace?

Money and Stewardship

Our piety and obedience to God, however, are marked by more than how we worship. United Methodists also have definite teachings about the use of money and the value of financial stewardship. Wesley created three rules for the use of money by Methodists: Earn all you can, save all you can, and give all you can.[5] The first rule, earn all you can, demonstrates Wesley's belief that honest, hard work was a way of participating in God's activity in the world and that people should be fairly compensated for their work. The second rule, save all you can, calls us to a simple lifestyle. Wesley warned us against extravagance, opulence, and self-gratification. He could not reconcile acquiring luxuries with the need to share with the poor. The world today is deeply divided between the rich and the poor. For the sake of others, United Methodists are called to observe simple and sustainable lifestyles. Give all you can, Wesley's third rule of stewardship, gives meaning to the first two rules. Earning and saving are preludes to giving to God. Wesley knew how to receive and how to give. Although he earned significant royalties through his book sales, Wesley lived throughout his life on the same amount of income he had at age twenty-five. He simply gave the additional earnings away![6] At his death, Wesley was carried to his grave by six paupers who were paid one pound each, the whole of his remaining savings. The draperies used in the sanctuary at Wesley's funeral service were sewn into dresses and donated to poor women.

Today United Methodists remain generous people. While our giving may be below what Wesley expected, many of us give generously to our local congregations and support financially the work of the denomination both regionally and globally. And when hurricanes and earthquakes strike, United Methodists give even more.

> What insights do you gain from Wesley's rules for the use of money? How might his thinking influence your use of money?

United Methodist Membership Vows

The Apostle Paul's words in Ephesians 4:1 to live as those who are worthy of God's call challenge and inspire us. Even so, a life focused on loving and serving others in the name of Jesus will not take shape automatically. Thank goodness, whenever United Methodists commit to becoming worthy of our calling, we discover that we are not alone. God's grace is present in all of our spiritual disciplines, empowering us to be ever more loving in our thoughts and actions. We are all recipients of God's love through Jesus Christ. Within a local church community and throughout the world via our connections, United Methodists continually respond to God's grace and reaffirm our commitment to love God and our neighbors more fully. With other followers of Jesus, we go forth to serve and transform our communities and world.

We invite you to claim or renew your commitment to live as a United Methodist Christian. You may have been United Methodist all of your life and now are even more convinced that you are in the right denomination. Or you may be exploring joining a local United Methodist congregation and believe that it is time to make a decision. In our journey of salvation, all of us need to recommit again and again to read our Bibles; be a part of the universal church; celebrate our history; affirm our distinctive characteristics; and finally do no harm, do good, and observe the spiritual disciplines in the midst of connectional believers such as United Methodists

If you would like to join a local congregation within The United Methodist Church, you may do so in one of several ways:

1. By profession of faith and baptism. If you are not yet a baptized Christian, discuss with a pastor the meaning of baptism and church membership, and continue your spiritual journey among the people called United Methodist.

2. By transfer from another Christian denomination. If you have previously been part of another denomination, we would welcome you as a United Methodist. Your new congregation will write for your letter of membership at your former congregation. Because you have already been baptized, baptism will not be repeated.

3. By transfer from another United Methodist congregation. If you wish to serve God in a new United Methodist congregation, at your request, your new church will write your former congregation for your letter of membership.

The baptismal covenant proclaims our adoption by God's grace into Christ's holy church and our promise to respond in faith and love. It provides the opportunity for people to renounce sin and profess Christian faith with the following questions asked on behalf of the universal church, the entire body of Christ:

Do you renounce the spiritual forces of wickedness, reject the evil powers of this world, and repent of your sin?

Do you accept the freedom and power God gives you to resist evil, injustice, and oppression in whatever forms they present themselves?

Do you confess Jesus Christ as your Savior, put your whole trust in his grace, and promise to serve him as your Lord, in union with the church which Christ has opened to people of all ages, nations, and races?[7]

What do these questions say to you about what it means to be a Christian? How do they inspire you or challenge you?

When joining The United Methodist Church, individuals are asked the following questions:

As members of Christ's universal church, will you be loyal to The United Methodist Church, and do all in your power to strengthen its ministries?...

As members of this congregation, will you faithfully participate in its ministries by your prayers, your presence, your gifts, your service, and your witness?[8]

What do these questions say to you about being a United Methodist Christian? How do they inspire or challenge you?

A Covenant Prayer

In 1755, Wesley celebrated the first covenant service in the Methodist movement. Finding the service rich and meaningful, Wesley celebrated the service at least once each year in every location. Wesley claimed, "It was an occasion for a variety of spiritual experiences.... I do not know that ever we had a greater blessing. Afterwards many desired to return thanks, either for a sense of pardon, for full salvation, or for a fresh manifestation of His graces, healing all their backslidings."[9]

The heart of the service was the Covenant Prayer, which invites persons to commit themselves to God. Over the years, Wesley's Covenant Prayer has been amended a number of times, primarily to update the language and to soften some of Wesley's expectations of his people. The following Covenant Prayer is the most well known. Read the words of Wesley's prayer as our invitation to you to continue your journey as a United Methodist Christian:

> I am no longer my own, but thine.
> Put me to what thou wilt, rank me with whom thou wilt.
> Put me to doing, put me to suffering.
> Let me be employed by thee or laid aside for thee,
> exalted for thee or brought low by thee.
> Let me be full, let me be empty.
> Let me have all things, let me have nothing.
> I freely and heartily yield all things
> to thy pleasure and disposal.
> And now, O glorious and blessed God,
> Father, Son, and Holy Spirit,
> thou art mine, and I am thine. So be it.
> And the covenant which I have made on earth,
> let it be ratified in heaven. Amen.[10]

Notes

1. *The Works of John Wesley,* vol. 9 (Nashville: Abingdon Press, 1989), pp. 67–75.

2. From *The Book of Discipline of The United Methodist Church 2008* (Nashville: The United Methodist Publishing House, 2008), ¶103, p. 72.

3. From *The Book of Discipline 2008,* p. 74.

4. "A Service of Word and Table I," *The United Methodist Hymnal* (Nashville: The United Methodist Publishing House, 1989), p. 7.

5. "The Use of Money" sermon. See *The Works of John Wesley,* vol. 2 (Nashville: Abingdon Press, 1985), p. 263–80.

6. Charles A. Sauer, *A Pocket Story of John Wesley* (Nashville: Tidings, 1967), pp. 102–3.

7. "The Baptismal Covenant I," *Hymnal,* pp. 32–49.

8. Ibid., p. 38. The 2008 General Conference added "and your witness."

9. January 1, 1775. From *The United Methodist Book of Worship* (Nashville: The United Methodist Publishing House, 1992), #288.

10. "A Covenant Prayer in the Wesleyan Tradition," *Hymnal,* # 607.

IF YOU WANT
TO KNOW MORE

The following resources will be helpful if you would like to study further about The United Methodist Church and what it means to be a United Methodist Christian.

Official Resources

The Book of Discipline of The United Methodist Church. Nashville: The United Methodist Publishing House, 2008.
The Book of Resolutions of The United Methodist Church. Nashville: The United Methodist Publishing House, 2008.
The United Methodist Hymnal. Nashville: The United Methodist Publishing House, 1989.
The United Methodist Book of Worship. Nashville: The United Methodist Publishing House, 1992.

Study Resources

Allen, Charles. *Meet the Methodists: An Introduction to The United Methodist Church.* Nashville: Abingdon Press, 1986, 1998.

Campbell, Ted. *Methodist Doctrine: The Essentials.* Nashville: Abingdon Press, 1999.

Felton, Gayle. *United Methodists and the Sacraments.* Nashville: Abingdon Press, 2007.

Maddox, Randy and John E. Vickers, eds. *The Cambridge Companion to John Wesley.* New York: Cambridge University Press, 2010.

Stokes, Mack. *Major United Methodist Beliefs.* Revised and enlarged edition. Nashville: Abingdon Press, 1998.

Watts, Ewart. *We Are United Methodists.* Revised edition. Nashville: Abingdon Press, 1998.

Willimon, William H. *This We Believe: The Core of Wesleyan Faith and Practice.* Nashville: Abingdon Press, 2010.

————. *Why I Am a United Methodist.* Nashville: Abingdon Press, 1990.

Yrigoyen, Charles, Jr. *Belief Matters: United Methodism's Doctrinal Standards.* Nashville: Abingdon Press, 2001.

Video Resource

What Does It Mean to Be United Methodist? Nashville: Abingdon Press, 2004. Video.

Helpful Links

Official website of The United Methodist Church, www.umc.org

The General Board of Discipleship of The United Methodist Church, www.gbod.org

The General Board of Church and Society of The United Methodist Church, www.umc-gbcs.org

The General Board of Global Ministries, www.gbgm-umc.org.

The General Board of Higher Education and Ministry, ww.gbhem.org.

LEADER HELPS
FOR
A SMALL-GROUP
STUDY

Living as United Methodist Christians

Pastors and local church leaders often ask: What do we offer as a way into church membership and into life as a United Methodist Christian? How do we help longtime United Methodists grow in faith as they explore what it means to be a United Methodist Christian? The study book *Living as United Methodist Christians: Our Story, Our Beliefs, Our Lives* is ideal for use by small groups or classes and by individual adults who wish to hear and claim for themselves the Christian story, the particular emphases of belief and practice of United Methodists, and ways to live as a United Methodist Christian.

Living as United Methodist Christians offers adults a "means of grace" or the opportunity to experience the active presence of God as they explore what it might mean to claim or to reclaim Christian life in a United Methodist congregation. It will not only help people learn *about* The United Methodist Church; it will *inspire them to claim for themselves* the redemptive love of God revealed through Jesus Christ as part of their entry into membership or their continuing participation in the life of the church. Both longtime United Methodists and newcomers who are considering membership can deepen their faith and grow in love and service of God and neighbor as they learn more about what it means to believe and live as United Methodist Christians.

Leading a *Living as United Methodist Christians* Small-Group Study

The role of a small-group leader for *Living as United Methodist Christians* is to prepare for and facilitate the group sessions in order to help people explore and reflect upon the topic. A leader is not expected to be an expert. In fact, a leader often learns along with the participants. All you need is provided in the study book. So what does a leader do?

A Leader Prepares

A small-group leader has some basic preparation responsibilities. They are:

• *Pray.* Ask for God's guidance as you prepare to lead the session.

• *Read and Reflect.* Review the session chapter, its Bible readings, and other resources or materials ahead of time. Jot down questions or insights that occur during your reading.

• *Think about Group Participants.* Who are the adults who might come to this group? What life issues do they have? What questions might they have? These adults may or may not come from a United Methodist background. They may have grown up in another Christian denomination or they may not have attended church at all. Whatever their background and whether they are newcomers or active members, they want to know more about

United Methodist views of the Bible and Christian faith. If they are new to the church, they may have come through marriage, because of their children, because of a life crisis, or for any number of reasons. Most come because they are looking for deeper meaning in their lives.

• *Prepare the Learning Area.* Gather any needed supplies, such as large sheets of paper, markers, paper and pencils, Bibles, audiovisual equipment, masking tape, a *Book of Discipline*, a *Book of Resolutions*, *The United Methodist Book of Worship*, *The United Methodist Hymnal*, and supplies needed for worship experiences. Make sure everyone will have a place to sit.

• *Pray for the Group Participants.* Before the participants arrive, pray for each one. Ask for God's blessing on your session. Offer thanks to God for the opportunity to lead the session.

A Leader Creates a Welcoming Atmosphere

Hospitality is a spiritual discipline. A leader helps create an environment that makes others feel welcome and helps every participant experience the freedom to ask questions and to state opinions. Such an atmosphere is based upon mutual respect.

• *Greet Participants as They Arrive.* Say aloud the name of each participant. If the class is meeting for the first time, use name tags.

• *Listen.* As group discussion unfolds, affirm the comments and ideas of participants. Avoid the temptation to dominate conversation or "correct" the ideas of participants.

• *Affirm.* Thank people for telling about what they think or feel. Acknowledge their contributions to discussion in positive ways, even if you disagree with their ideas.

Session Plans

CHAPTER 1

What Is Our Biblical Story?

Focus: United Methodist Christians affirm the authority of the Holy Bible as the source of our understanding about God and God's relationship with us.

Scripture: *"Every scripture is inspired by God and is useful for teaching, for showing mistakes, for correcting, and for training character, so that the person who belongs to God can be equipped to do everything that is good." (2 Timothy 3:16-17)*

OPEN THE SESSION

Read aloud the title, the chapter focus, and the Scripture verses. Ask: What questions arise for you from the title, the focus for the chapter, and the Scripture verses? List questions on a large sheet of paper or a markerboard.

EXPLORE THE CHAPTER

Review the Reading

Review highlights of each section of chapter 1. Invite participants to respond to the questions at the end of each section. Review the list of questions. Invite participants to offer any insights or ideas that might address questions on the list.

Suggested Activities

Have a Bible Study. Form teams of two or three. Assign the teams one or more of the following Scriptures: Genesis 1–4; Exodus 3:1-17; Isaiah 11:1-9; Micah 6:8; Luke 4:16-10; John 3:16-17;

Revelation 22:1-5. Tell each team to read the assigned Scripture and discuss the following questions: What do these Scriptures say to you about God? about human beings? about God's relationship with human beings? Have them share highlights of their discussions with the entire group.

Share Personal Stories of God's Grace. Review highlights of the section "The Biblical Message of God's Grace." Invite participants to share examples of God's grace at work in their lives or in the lives of people they know.

CLOSE THE SESSION

Give the Reading Assignment: Encourage participants to read chapter 2, "What Do We Share with Other Christians?" Tell them to write responses to the questions at the end of each section and to make note of questions they might have about the reading.

Pray Together. Invite participants to name prayer concerns and joys. Pray together the prayer at the end of the chapter or one of your own.

CHAPTER 2
What Do We Share with Other Christians?

Focus: United Methodist Christians understand themselves as part of Christ's universal church in the world.

Scripture: *"Christ is just like the human body—a body is a unit and has many parts; and all the parts of the body are one body, even though there are many. We were all baptized by one Spirit into one body." (1 Corinthians 12:12-13)*

OPEN THE SESSION

Read aloud the title, the chapter focus, and the Scripture verses. Ask: What questions arise for you from your reading this week or from the focus for the chapter? List questions on a large sheet of paper or a markerboard.

EXPLORE THE CHAPTER

Review the Reading

Review highlights of each section of chapter 2. Invite participants to tell about responses they made to the questions at the end of each section. Review the list of questions. Invite participants to offer any insights or ideas that might address questions on the list.

Suggested Activities

Do a Bible Study. Have participants form teams of two or three. Tell the teams to read 1 Corinthians 12 and discuss the following questions: What words or phrases stand out for you? Why? What does the reading say to you about God's vision for how human beings can live together? What connections do you see between this reading and Wesley's view of the universal church? Have the teams share highlights of their conversations with the entire group

Discuss Creeds. Have participants form two teams. Give each team a copy of *The United Methodist Hymnal*. Tell team one to read "The Nicene Creed" (880) and team two to read "The Apostles' Creed" (881–882). Have each team discuss the following questions: What stands out for you in this creed? Why? What does the creed say to you about God? about Jesus? about the Holy Spirit? What challenges you or inspires you?

CLOSE THE SESSION

Give the Reading Assignment: Encourage participants to read chapter 3, "What Is Our United Methodist Story?" Tell them to write responses to the questions at the end of each section and to make note of questions they might have about the reading.

Pray Together. Invite participants to name prayer concerns and joys. Pray together the prayer at the end of the chapter or one of your own.

CHAPTER 3

What Is Our United Methodist Story?

Focus: United Methodist Christians emerged from a movement dedicated to spreading scriptural holiness.

Scripture: *"So then let's also run the race that is laid out in front of us, since we have such a great cloud of witnesses surrounding us. Let's throw off any extra baggage, get rid of the sin that trips us up, and fix our eyes on Jesus, the pioneer and perfecter of our faith."* (Hebrews 12:1-2)

OPEN THE SESSION

Read aloud the title, the chapter focus, and the Scripture verses. Ask: What questions arise for you from your reading this week or from the focus for the chapter? List questions on a large sheet of paper or a markerboard.

EXPLORE THE CHAPTER

Review the Reading

Review highlights of each section of chapter 3. Invite participants to tell about responses they made to the questions at the end of each section. Review the list of questions. Invite participants to offer any insights or ideas that might address questions on the list.

Suggested Activities

Discuss the Wesley Family. Ask the following questions: What particularly struck you about John Wesley's life and family?

Why? Continue by asking these questions from the section "John Wesley": How do you think Wesley's parents and family life contributed to his role as the leader of the Methodist movement? How do you see the role of your family and upbringing in your faith journey?

Reflect on the Aldersgate Experience. Read aloud John Wesley's description of his experience of assurance at Aldersgate. Ask: Since Wesley was so devoted to scriptural holiness, does his experience surprise you? Why or why not? Have you had an experience similar to his? If so, what was it like? See also *Book of Discipline*, pp. 9–20.

Create a Timeline. Provide the group with markers and a long sheet of white paper. Tell them to create a timeline of Methodism in America. Tell them to refer to the material in the chapter. Encourage them to either draw or write about events as they create the timeline. When they are finished, ask: What stood out for you? What challenged you or made you curious? Why?

CLOSE THE SESSION

Give the Reading Assignment: Encourage participants to read chapter 4, "What Do United Methodists Believe?" Tell them to write responses to the questions at the end of each section and to make note of questions they might have about the reading.

Pray Together. Invite participants to name prayer concerns and joys. Pray together the prayer at the end of the chapter or one of your own.

CHAPTER 4
What Do United Methodists Believe?

Focus: United Methodists emphasize the Christian belief that God's grace, the undeserved, unmerited, and loving action of God, permeates our lives.

Scripture: *"While he was still a long way off, his father saw him and was moved with compassion. His father ran to him, hugged him, and kissed him. Then his son said, 'Father, I have sinned against heaven and against you. I no longer deserve to be called your son.' But the father said to his servants, 'Quickly, bring out the best robe and put it on him! Put a ring on his finger and sandals on his feet! Fetch the fattened calf and slaughter it. We must celebrate with feasting because this son of mine was dead and has come back to life! He was lost and is found!' And they began to celebrate." (Luke 15:20-24)*

OPEN THE SESSION

Read aloud the title, the chapter focus, and the Scripture verses. Ask: What questions arise for you from your reading this week or from the focus for the chapter? List questions on a large sheet of paper or a markerboard.

EXPLORE THE CHAPTER

Review the Reading

Review highlights of each section of chapter 4. Invite participants to tell about responses they made to the questions at the end of each section. Review the list of questions. Invite participants to offer any insights or ideas that might address questions on the list. See also *Book of Discipline*, pp. 41–86.

Suggested Activities

Discuss Wesley's View of Grace. Review highlights of "Prevenient Grace," "Justifying Grace," and "Sanctifying Grace." Ask: What insights do you gain through this description of God's grace at work in our lives? What challenges you or inspires you? What connections do you see between this description of grace and God's salvation?

Consider Faith and Works. Review the sections "Practical Divinity" and "Faith and Good Works." Ask: How do you understand the relationship between what we believe and what we do on a daily basis? How do our good works relate to our salvation? to our belief in God's grace at work in our lives?

CLOSE THE SESSION

Give the Reading Assignment. Encourage participants to read chapter 5, "How Do United Methodists Serve God and Neighbor?" Tell them to write responses to the questions at the end of each section and to make note of questions they might have about the reading.

Pray Together. Invite participants to name prayer concerns and joys. Pray together the prayer at the end of the chapter or one of your own.

CHAPTER 5
How Do United Methodists Serve God and Neighbor?

Focus: United Methodists organize in ways that support a ministry of love and service to God and to one another.

Scripture: *"Then the king will say to those on his right, 'Come, you who will receive good things from my Father. Inherit the kingdom that was prepared for you before the world began. I was hungry and you gave me food to eat. I was thirsty and you gave me a drink. I was a stranger and you welcomed me. I was naked and you gave me clothes to wear. I was sick and you took care of me. I was in prison and you visited me.'*

"Then those who are righteous will reply to him, 'Lord, when did we see you hungry and feed you, or thirsty and give you a drink? When did we see you as a stranger and welcome you, or naked and give you clothes to wear? When did we see you sick or in prison and visit you?'

"Then the king will reply to them, 'I assure you that when you have done it for one of the least of these brothers and sisters of mine, you have done it for me.'" (Matthew 25:34-40)

OPEN THE SESSION

Read aloud the title, the chapter focus, and the Scripture verses. Ask: What questions arise for you from your reading this week or from the focus for the chapter? List questions on a large sheet of paper or a markerboard.

EXPLORE THE CHAPTER

Review the Reading

Review highlights of each section of chapter 5. Invite participants to tell about responses they made to the questions at the end of each section. Review the list of questions. Invite participants to offer any insights or ideas that might address questions on the list.

Suggested Activities

Do a Bible Study. Have participants form teams of two or three. Tell the teams to read Matthew 25:34-40 and "The Outward Journey" in the study book. Ask: What does this Scripture say to you about how to live out your faith? How does it speak to contemporary culture? Tell the teams to continue discussion by responding to the question at the end of the section: How does Matthew 25:34-40 speak to you about a balance between the inward and outward journeys of faith?

Consider the General Rules. Review highlights of the section "Faith into Action." Discuss the questions at the end of this section: How do you respond to Wesley's General Rules to do no harm, do good, and attend to the ordinances of God? What connections do you see between these rules and the idea of putting faith into action? See also *Book of Discipline*, ¶103, pp. 73ff.

Discuss the Social Creed. Read aloud "The Social Creed" included in this chapter. Ask the question at the end of this section: What challenges you or inspires you in the Social Creed? Continue by discussing the following question: How do you see the principles in the Social Creed at work in our world?

CLOSE THE SESSION

Give the Reading Assignment: Encourage participants to read chapter 6, "How Do United Methodists Live and Worship?" Tell them to write responses to the questions at the end of each section and to make note of questions they might have about the reading.

Pray Together. Invite participants to name prayer concerns and joys. Pray together the prayer at the end of the chapter or one of your own.

CHAPTER 6
How Do United Methodists Live and Worship?

Focus: United Methodist Christians celebrate God's salvation and grace in Jesus Christ, practice spiritual disciplines, and put Christian belief into daily practice.

Scripture: *"I encourage you to live as people worthy of the call you received from God. Conduct yourselves with all humility, gentleness, and patience. Accept each other with love, and make an effort to preserve the unity of the Spirit with the peace that ties you together. You are one body and one spirit just as God also called you in one hope. There is one Lord, one faith, one baptism, and one God and Father of all who is over all, through all, and in all." (Ephesians 4:1-6)*

OPEN THE SESSION

Read aloud the title, the chapter focus, and the Scripture verses. Ask: What questions arise for you from your reading this week or from the focus for the chapter? List questions on a large sheet of paper or a markerboard. Tell participants that this final chapter will invite them to consider more personally how they might grow in faith as they consider what it means to be a United Methodist Christian. It will provide them the opportunity to reflect prayerfully on spiritual disciplines, the profession of faith, and membership vows. Be sure to allow adequate time at the close of the session for prayerful reflection.

EXPLORE THE CHAPTER

Review the Reading

Review highlights of each section of chapter 6. Invite participants to tell about responses they made to the questions at the end of each section. Review the list of questions. Invite participants to offer any insights or ideas that might address questions on the list.

Suggested Activities

Examine Spiritual Disciplines. Create a poster that lists the spiritual disciplines named in the section "Observing Spiritual Disciplines." Display so that all can easily see the list. Tell participants to silently reflect on the following questions: Which disciplines mean most to you? Which disciplines might you observe more frequently? How do you think these disciplines or practices might enrich your life and your continuing spiritual growth? Invite participants to share their reflections with the entire group if they feel moved to do so.

Discuss Baptism and Communion. Review highlights of

the section "Holy Communion and Baptism." If you have time, have participants look at the services in *The United Methodist Hymnal*. Invite participants to ask questions they might have about these sacraments. Ask the questions at the end of this section: What thoughts or feelings do you have about the way United Methodists practice Holy Communion and baptism? How do you connect the practices with God's grace?

Explore Membership Vows. Review highlights of the section "United Methodist Membership Vows." Invite questions or comments from the participants about the profession of faith and the local church membership vows. Ask the questions at the end of this section: What do these questions say to you about what it means to be a Christian? How do they inspire you or challenge you?

CLOSE THE SESSION

Share Insights from the Study. Invite participants to share insights or inspiration they gained from this study of *Living as United Methodist Christians*. Thank everyone for participating in the study. Invite them to read further information in the resources listed in the study book. Encourage any in your group who wish to make a profession of faith or to become members of your congregation to talk with the pastor.

Pray Together. Invite all the participants to prayerfully and silently consider what the next step in their faith journey might be. Allow a few moments for silent prayer. Close this time by reading aloud the Covenant Prayer at the end of the chapter.